Practical Floor Supervision:

A Hands-On Guide for Warehouse Supervisors

Paul Lukehart

Table of Contents

Why You're Reading This

Being a warehouse supervisor is tough. You're caught between the hourly employees on the floor and higher management. You need to meet production and quality goals, all while maintaining a safe environment and keeping the team playing nice together. Your shift probably runs either early or late. Your training may have been 3 months of shadowing or a week or two of doing the process and then being out on your own to figure it out. You may have been an hourly employee for years, or you may be fresh out of college. There may be no training at all, but you're now the boss and leader in charge of getting it done.

I was in a similar situation. When I got out of the Army, I went to work for Target and then for Amazon, both of which have large-scale, well-established, well-resourced distribution operations. The training programs for each of these environments varied, but the common thread was that, although both taught quite a lot of about some of the processes within the warehouse, the actual mechanics and lessons of how to be an effective floor supervisor were imparted largely by experience and word-of-mouth instead of being collected in a manual or consolidated source. I learned from the overall on-boarding process, shadowing, asking questions of the other supervisors, and by a lot of self-learning and trial-and-error.

This handbook book exists because as I moved through floor leadership roles in warehousing, I noticed certain expectations, tricks, tools, processes, or techniques that were more useful than others. In fact, without them, supervisors missed big pieces of how to be effective on the floor. These things—these fundamentals and processes—were never written down in one place, but understanding them was essential to succeeding as a floor supervisor.

When I moved from the large organizations to smaller ones, I noticed that many supervisors were not aware of those techniques, either from lack of exposure or by not really noticing them. It's hard to know how to coach hourly employees on quality or productivity when those things aren't defined, or when you've never had someone coach you on a process for effective performance management.

When I noticed the "experience deficiency," I started to look for something I could put in their hands to lay out, in a digestible format, what they should be doing – what the mechanics of the job were. As I looked for literature on warehousing, I saw any number of high-level books, but most of them were focused on things like setting up the warehouse, picking the correct equipment, assessing whether or not to automate, how to develop financials and productivity metrics, and so on. All of those things are important in running a successful operation and framing ideas for larger initiatives, but they don't paint a good picture for the floor-level supervisor who's trying get the pallet of onions from the Receiving dock into the right 53' trailer.

Further, it became apparent that fundamentals and mechanics **do** have to be taught. They are not instinctive to many supervisors or managers, and they must be pointed out. The way this usually happens is by acquiring experience, or "developing" subordinates or peers to do what needs doing. This often happens during an introductory "shadowing" period at a warehouse, where the new supervisor follows around someone who has learned the techniques for getting things done. This is sometimes called "mentoring," and mentors have varying degrees of patience and expertise to share with the new guy. Having the newbie is fun for a few days but quickly turns into extra work that the mentor doesn't want.

As a result, every new supervisor ends up re-inventing the wheel to some degree to figure out how to do things right. Experience is a very slow teacher on its own, while learning from others' experience is an extremely powerful tool.

I had a retrospective "a-ha" moment when I, wondering why my current supervisors were not doing some of what I considered to be basic supervisory "stuff," recalled an area manager I knew at Amazon describing the pre-work that went into getting a shift ready for start-up. He would do his staffing roster for the next day when he completed his current day, and then would come in early to ensure that there were adequate RF guns in the start-up area and that some of the other equipment was ready; that the lead was present and knew what the assignments would be; and had his notes for start-up prepared. No one told him to do this. He'd learned by trial and error from getting spanked after difficult shifts where things went wrong.

I had done some similar things in previous roles myself, but it struck me that there was very little documentation on how to get a shift ready. He had come up with his pre-shift routine - his standard work - himself and was very successful.

Most of what's in this handbook is very straightforward, easy stuff to accomplish, like getting equipment and notes ready before the shift. Yet when I went to a smaller operation, many of the supervisors and applicants were from environments where that kind of preparation was unknown. Not only was the performance absent, but it took a while for the operations managers to realize what the supervisors weren't doing!

At that point, I figured, Why not take basic learnings like that and capture them in a format for supervisors who haven't been exposed (at all, or for very long) to world-class operations environments. We needed to have a consolidated list of fundamentals for supervisors that is concise, easy to reference and understand, and most importantly, **actionable for immediate results** in team management, quality, productivity, and general priorities in approaching the job. This is what I'd want my supervisors to know and do.

The guide will cover a little bit about warehousing in general for anyone who has not yet entered or is considering the roles. It will then go into some basics on a process-orientation, shift structure, key metrics, and team management. This is to help you understand the significance of what's going on in each key area from a performance and operations perspective. Each section will have some introductory framing, some theory or "why this is important," and then **actions to take** to improve or help other people.

This book will be most useful for supervisors who have had limited exposure to formal training, or for anyone who is moving into warehousing or logistics functions or industries. It will also be useful for more experienced leadership at a facility level to conduct supervisor development and identify gaps in the existing operation.

It is a tactical guide to operating for warehouse supervisors.

Warehousing

No kid ever told his parents "Mom and Dad, I want to work in a warehouse when I'm a grown-up!"

A Brief Overview of Warehouse Supervision As An Occupation

Industry Overview

Distribution, as a subset of logistics, is a huge industry. Every single physical product that you or your neighbor did not personally make had to be moved from somewhere to get to you. Your clothing had to be shipped by container and truck from foreign factories; your food had to be put on trucks or trains to get across the country to you; the beef jerky or pens or kitchen utensils that you purchased from Amazon had to be moved to Amazon from China, and then sent out again to you by USPS.

All companies of all sizes that have a physical product engage in physical distribution. Some of these operations are more sophisticated than others and use varying degrees of automation to increase internal efficiencies. Some are very small warehouses that may send out only a couple of trucks per day, and rely on paper-pick systems to get orders out the door, and some send out hundreds of trucks to service stores with automated picking in a hub-and-spoke and goods-to-picker model.

A warehouse or distribution facility will typically have hourly employees, a first-level supervisor, a shift or department manager (or a manager that serves as both roles), and then depending on the size of the building, another senior manager, and then the General Manager.

Warehouses are typically located to minimize cost of transportation to customers, which means that they are often not in some of the highly desirable locales. With the wide range of distribution and storage, the geographic locations available are very flexible. You're likely to find significant warehousing opportunities in small towns to mid-size cities near transportation hubs (think Lexington, KY; Phoenix, AZ; Bakersfield, CA; Jacksonville, FL, etc.) as well as marquee port cities like San Francisco or New York. Chicago, Houston, LA, Memphis, and

Houston are huge logistics hubs. However, the warehouses, as you might expect, are not in the downtown areas, and are instead usually located in industrial parks or less-pleasant parts of town.

Companies large enough to look at optimizing transportation cost will also likely look at labor laws, tax rates, and other variables in deciding where to locate, which is why some distribution hubs are located in the middle of nowhere (hello, Nevada!).

What this means is that the whole industry has immense employment opportunity at many levels, from floor-level leadership to upper management, across a wide range of geographic locations.

However, there are some things that you should be aware of before getting into the industry.

Desirability

Adam Smith wrote that:

"The five following are the principal circumstances which, so far as I have been able to observe, make up for a small pecuniary gain in some employments, and counterbalance a great one in others. First, the agreeableness of disagreeableness of the employments themselves; secondly, the easiness and cheapness, or the difficulty and expense of learning them; thirdly, the constancy or inconstancy of employment in them; fourthly, the small or great trust which must be reposed in those who exercise them; and fifthly, the probability or improbability of success in them."

While he wrote that to frame the discussion of wages in different jobs, looking at warehouse supervision in these terms indicates that it is largely an agreeable employment for its compensation. It is busy, detail- and results-oriented, and has schedules that are sometimes difficult (e.g., 4x10-hr night-shifts is not an uncommon schedule). There is not a lot of "office work" per se – there is administrative paper-shuffling, record-keeping, and administration that must be done, but the administrative stuff is to support the real work and is not the work itself. Distribution is a cost-center for all businesses, so there is not tremendous upside to operating; you can't make money, but you can lose less of it.

To summarize those factors as they apply to warehousing supervision:

Factor	Notes
Agreeableness/ Disagreeableness	Steady Schedule, little travel; Shift Work can be monotonous and results-oriented, with bosses that are largely metric-driven. Not much social opportunity. Development & exposure highly dependent on who the supervisors in the building are. Not a very "creative" environment. Local culture can make for an intense 0-defect workplace. Warehousing/distribution is not a "highly desired" profession, resulting in lower talent levels than other professions.
Cost of Learning	Minimal; development usually conducted as On-the-Job Training (OJT) after initial introductory training; Requires attention to detail to learn local systems and processes
Constancy of Employment	Very steady; widespread opportunity. Can be seasonal. Usually a 4-day, 10- or 12-hr/day workweek for floor supervision. Can require odd hours and many hours depending on the operation and season.
Responsibility/Scope	Responsible for safety, performance, and output of hourly employees in a process as well as administrative tasks and projects. Scope is bounded by company policies/processes.
Success / Opportunity	Extensive within distribution industry; local opportunity may be limited by your facility's structure. Frequent

	turnover due to shift work, hours, perceived opportunity in current facility, and local leadership environment.

Depending on experience, pay can run (as of about 2019) from $45-$70k+ for supervisors, depending on the size of the operation and the experience of the individual. Pay is generally good compared with experience-comparable opportunities. Supervisors can oversee shifts from ~10 to 100-200 hourly employees, depending again on the facility, business, and seasonality.

Volatility

Supervisor positions are also typically not very volatile if you perform to some basic standards. Distribution is a large and growing industry, and qualified leaders will be able to find jobs for years from now as long as physical products are still moved from one place to another. With the e-commerce goods-to-consumer model disrupting much traditional retail and moving inventory closer to consumers, the distribution requirement will continue to grow. A competent distribution supervisor is well-equipped to find work in a variety of places and industries.

Warehousing Flow

Warehouses typically have several main functions, or departments, that are tied to the flow of product through the warehouse.

They first must *Receive* product, which is the physical process of removing product from the inbound shipping vehicle and putting it systematically and physically within the warehouse's inventory. This is usually done on a truck dock of some sort. It can be a manually completed process or it can use a whole variety of scanners, conveyors, and other automation to pull the product out of the shipping vehicle, label it, and receive it into inventory.

Then the product has to be *put away* and stored until needed. This can be called *Putaway*, *Stowing*, *Stocking,* or other names, but the function is the same.

Then the product needs to be moved on demand to the outbound docks- also known as *Picking* – where it is *Packed* or prepared for shipping, for the consumer. Then it goes to the shipping truck or container and is sent from the facility to the next step. This is *Loading* or *Shipping*.

Receiving and Putaway are *Inbound* functions. Picking and Shipping are *Outbound* functions. Departments are usually organized around one or more of these core functions. Sometimes they are organized by times of day if the facility has fixed shipping and receiving cut-offs and can shift labor between departments.

These functions typically have system transactions associated with them, which means that they can be measured for productivity purposes. Each of the processes within the major functions can have a variety of sub-processes to ensure quality, accuracy, and maintain a high level of productivity. Picking, for example, receives a tremendous amount of attention and thought intended to optimize productivity for a department that by itself can take 40% of a building's labor hours.

Other departments in warehouses can include Inventory Management or Quality Control functions, Maintenance, IT, Safety, Returns/Reverse Logistics, or other specialty functions depending on the business.

Automation

Automation will cause mass reduction in required headcount in warehousing and distribution jobs. In some cases, as in goods-to-picker systems, or cutting-edge facilities, this is already the case. However, forklift drivers and the people who supervise them will still be required for many years. The sheer variety of product and process flows right now is a barrier to complete industry displacement of labor, though levels of automation are increasing in variety and scope.

That said, many of the processes can and will be automated. The most advanced systems are in material moving technology, like Automated Storage and Retrieval Systems (ASRS), goods-to-picker robotics like Kiva, and co-bots like 6-River Systems to minimize fixed infrastructure. Even truck loading and unloading robotics are being deployed. This means that putaway and picking are probably the first processes to be automated. Receiving and shipping, depending on the type of product, may be next. The major barrier in those processes is the type of product, but artificial intelligence, machine vision, and improved articulating arms are coming onto the markets. But until that becomes commonplace and cheap, people will be needed to manipulate product into and out of trailers and containers and input data.

Shifts

When you go to a supermarket or store, you expect that the shelves are stocked with what you need. Similarly, unlike the 6-8 week delivery of old-time cereal redemption prizes, we now expect delivery of items within a week, if not days, and soon within hours. As a result, warehouses and distribution centers frequently operate 22 or 24 hours per day, 7 days per week.

Most facilities staff to deal with this by having multiple shifts, which schedules typically being a 3-4 day / week, 10-12 hr/day schedule for the hourly employees. Production and Shift Supervisors and managers will typically come in about 30 minutes before the start of a shift and leave 30 minutes or an hour after shift. This makes the expectation of a 50-hr actual workweek realistic, with actual amounts depending somewhat on the individual facility. The long weekends are largely standard, and are an unadvertised perk of the industry, but the long-feeling weeks (frequently spent walking around a warehouse in a stressful environment) make you earn them.

The different shifts have different characteristics. Weekday shifts are busier because senior management and more Human Resources coverage is in the building. They will be looking into operational details, conducting projects and initiatives, and having meetings to address internal processes or respond to even higher-level management initiatives. Crossover shifts, where the front-half of the week and back-half of the week ("front and back half") overlap, will be very busy with meetings because that is the only day where all or most leadership is in the building.

Nights will, of course, go overnight, which is a difficult shift to adjust to. But the absence of most daytime management presence allows more latitude to execute the way you want to do things, within process boundaries. On the downside, there are less organizational resources available at night (e.g. HR, technical support, etc) to deal with problems or escalate issues.

Weekends are similar to nights, but will typically overlap into the week, increasing access to management and other resources.

So the most desirable shift will depend on what you want to do in distribution - do you want a high-visibility, high pressure environment, or do you prefer to operate on your own? Your shift will to some degree bound your ability to advance in your facility, as access to management and projects will shape the visibility senior management has on you.

Social Circles and Networking

Socially, warehouse supervision is not a "sexy" profession, and affords relatively little potential to build outside connections within the context of the job. It is very likely and possible to network with other members of your company as a member of the distribution operations team. Company operations and distribution networks are frequently close-knit. But if you are looking for wide contacts and building wide social and professional networks, then warehousing and distribution may not be your cup of tea. Higher level management gets the opportunity to build professional networks in the community through vendors and interaction with upstream and downstream customers, but the supervisor typically has limited interaction outside the building.

Your Job

Your role will be to manage a team administratively, ensure safety, quality, and productivity goals are met, and ensure that the employees have a positive working environment. Ultimately, you're supporting your employees, so they can do their best work to support your customer.

But how, exactly?

Fundamentals Overview

Warehouse supervisors need to be constantly aware of the operations fundamental "Big Three" priorities – Safety, Quality, and Productivity, in that order. The fundamentals are not so much practices as they are priorities - things to be aware of and on which to base decisions.

There are a lot of pressures to go the other way around, to worry about productivity first, then quality, then safety. Productivity numbers show up in daily reports. Behaviors that affect quality and safety don't show up in production reports. Rather, they don't until it's too late to correct the issue, and by then you have irritated customers or hurt employees.

The priorities are about setting the conditions for success. If you base your decisions on Safety, Quality, and Productivity, in that order, and understand that your job is to set those conditions and remove barriers for your team, you will succeed and even excel.

The following sections have brief overviews along with references, metrics, and techniques for effectiveness in each area.

Safety

Safety is first because it is essential to the successful operation of any distribution (or any) business – and, of course, putting the welfare of employees that are trusting in you first is absolutely the right thing to do. Your team will not be productive in an unsafe environment, and you don't want to go home after an accident knowing that you knew better and could have done something to prevent a serious injury or death.

Impacts

Safety incidents' impacts include employee injury- people can lose limbs or become seriously maimed or disfigured from safety incidents. These are life-changing events that you can mitigate or prevent. What are some other impacts?

There are business impacts: Every time there is an incident and investigation, you spend time - your time, the employee's time, HR's time, the safety team's time, and maybe other management time. This is expensive. You may have to send the employee for a drug test, particularly if equipment or property was damaged. This is expensive in both wages, cost of testing, and opportunity cost - what else could you have been doing?

Repairing property is expensive. From the employee-care perspective, Workers' Comp claims are expensive, and insurance for an accident-prone site is expensive. Paying for light duty or other non-productive functions is expensive. Having OSHA conduct more site investigations is expensive. The reputational and brand damage to companies is expensive. The recruiting cost of having to overcome an unsafe reputation is expensive.

A single incident, even with no one hurt and no property damage, can cost your company hundreds or thousands of dollars that can be saved by taking the time and effort to be safe. Savings are of course secondary to making sure everyone leaves in the same vehicle they came in, but it is an important consideration. Being safe has a definite payback in addition to being the right thing to do.

Safety Basics

Occupational safety is important enough and has enough specialized knowledge that facilities regularly have Safety Managers to deal with the administrative and structural aspects of the safety programs. They will be good resources for any questions that you have about workplace safety, although their direct role in influencing safety with your hourly employees may be limited. This means that **you** have to drive the safety culture.

The Occupational Safety and Health Administration (OSHA) is the judge of Safety in the workplace, and 29 CFR is the law. Its website is the repository of virtually all regulation and FAQs needed as guidance for a given environment. In warehousing we are particularly concerned with 29 CFR (Code of Federal Regulations) 1910 for Occupational Safety and Health Standards. Part 1904 deals with recording and reporting occupational injuries and illnesses, which is applicable as you start filling out safety incident reports on accidents and near-misses, and recommending countermeasures. 29 CFR gives legal standards for safety standards such as Lockout/Tagout, Personal Protective Equipment, Occupational Noise Exposure, Powered Industrial Trucks, etc. It's important to be aware of these because all of the safety training at your facility will be derived from these standards.

Here are some relevant basics about Occupational Safety.

OSHA articulates the difference between unsafe *actions*, *behaviors*, and *conditions*, and presents a *hierarchy of controls*.

According to OSHA, an "accident" is an unplanned, undesired event which may or may not result in injury or property damage, that interferes with the completion of an assigned task. A "Near Miss" is a form of an accident that does not result in injury or property damage. An "unsafe act" occurs when a worker ignores or is not aware of a standard operating procedure or safe work practice designed to protect the worker and prevent accidents. An "unsafe condition" is a hazardous condition or circumstance that could lead directly to an accident.

Once an accident occurs, you will investigate the incident. This involves fact-finding about the accident, interviewing the employees involved, and researching relevant procedures and standards. A useful technique for investigating is a re-enactment of the accident (without any damage or injury) with the employee while asking questions to determine why the events occurred. Generally you will fill out a report form to describe the incident, causes, and countermeasures. More detail is better than less in determining root causes. Taking pictures with elaborate detail about exactly what occurred is the best way to complete a fact-finding investigation.

Supervisors often conduct superficial investigations and write a short report just to get the assigned task done and get back into the rest of the shift. This is because investigating and writing is a pain in the butt. It takes time and attention that is needed elsewhere in production. However, half-stepping investigations and providing inadequate reports makes them useless in identifying and fixing unsafe conditions or behaviors.

Here are two examples of the same incident written up - not a safety incident per se, but an incident involving property damage from PIT:

"My Tablet slid off the center piece of pallet jack, therefore it fell on the floor and before I could stop I ran over it by accident"

And:

"At approximately 12:45 AM, the Team Member [TM] was moving a pallet of oranges from aisle 30 to load at TD11 using Pallet Jack #4. The TM took a picture of the pallet in the Truck with the tablet per FQA procedures, and placed the tablet on the top of the pallet jack's battery compartment. As the TM exited the truck trailing forks and looking in his direction of travel, the impact from going over the dock plate cause the tablet to jostle loose and fall from the top of the battery compartment. The TM began turning the pallet jack and caught the tablet under one of the fork's caster wheels, where it was crushed. The TM realized that he had run over something and stopped to investigate, where he discovered the crushed tablet. He reported the incident to his supervisor."

Which one was more effective in painting a picture that could be used for risk reduction and assessing the need for corrective action or countermeasures? The first offers virtually no detail that could be used to develop ways to avoid future incidents. The second identifies facts that lead to behavioral, procedural, and mechanical or engineering solutions to avoid future occurrences. Your incident descriptions should tend toward the second level of detail.

The OSHA material on Worksite Hazard Analysis is also very valuable knowledge in addressing the safety environment pre- and post-accident. Much of this information is available online at www.osha.gov.

The hierarchy of controls from most to least effective includes:

Engineering Controls: Designing the environment and job to eliminate hazards (e.g. lowering a rack to within employees' reach)

Safe Work Practices: Standard Operating Procedures for avoiding hazards (e.g. implementing Stop And Honk at intersections for PIT)

Administrative Controls: Other measures outside of the process to reduce factors that reduce safety (e.g. regular breaks, job rotation)

Personal Protective Equipment: When other methods cannot reduce hazards sufficiently, using protective equipment to reduce hazards (e.g. using gloves to handle pallets)

Your facility and business will also be tracking each and every safety occurrence, whether OSHA-recordable or not, in order to develop a more comprehensive safety program.

Warehousing

Warehousing is a higher-risk environment than many others due to the quantities of physical product being moved around. Being around Powered Industrial Trucks (PIT - Forklifts, pallet-jacks, etc), pallets high overhead, and automation (conveyors, belts, etc) creates hazards where serious injuries can happen. Safety records are measured as TRIR, or **Total Recordable Incident Rate**, which is calculated for a given period as:

$$\frac{\#\ Recordable\ Incidents * 200,000}{\#\ Hours\ worked\ by\ all\ employees} = TRIR$$

To put the level of risk in perspective, foundries as an industry have an OSHA recordable rate of 8.6 in 2013 (http://www.bls.gov/iif/oshwc/osh/os/ostb3958.pdf) , Computer manufacturing had a rate of .6, working at a gasoline station had a rate of 2.4, florists had a rate of .4, and warehousing and storage had a rate of 5.2.

OSHA Rate Examples

Industry	Rate
Florists	0.4
Gasoline Stations	2.4
Foundries	8.6
Computer manufacturing	0.6
Warehousing	5.2

The general safety ranges indicate that warehousing is – as might be expected – more dangerous than most office jobs, but not as dangerous as other heavy industrial work.

From a more utilitarian perspective, creating a safe work environment pays dividends directly by reducing Workers' Comp claims, OSHA investigations, and other costs of business. Investigations are a distraction from the core business of moving things from Point A to Point B, and the best way to avoid investigations is to have a safe workplace in the first place. Indirect benefits are high too and contribute to fewer employee issues like turnover, complaints, and general relations. An unsafe workplace drives people out because it creates unease and dissatisfaction.

Additionally, Safety has a sort of "incident-funnel" where there are many near-misses, some significant incidents, and a few serious incidents.

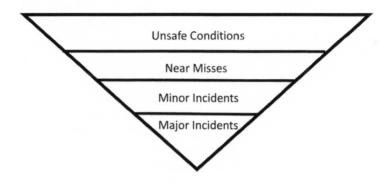

Serious safety incidents can be catastrophic to the business. If an employee dies in an accident, the rest of the team will be traumatized. The entire business can be in jeopardy from subsequent investigations and possible shut-downs until the cause is remedied, and that's not even mentioning lawsuits or the resulting negative publicity. Although these incidents have identifiable factors, the proximate causes are not always obvious to the people who engage in risky behaviors or cause unsafe conditions.

It's important to address even the minor safety conditions and incidents like "near-misses" because some percentage of those will turn into serious incidents. You've probably walked hundreds or thousands of miles safely, but there is always some risk of falling and knocking your head open on the sidewalk. It's the same in the warehouse, where someone who doesn't stop and honk at a doorway may be fine doing it a thousand times, but the thousand-and-first results in collision and amputation of another operator's limb. Addressing the conditions is very important in reducing risk of catastrophic events.

And yet even with all these compelling reasons to be very proactive and engaging with safety, and with many factors affecting safety conditions readily identified, safety is very difficult to manage and promote in the workplace. Why is that, and how can safety be managed effectively?

There are multiple barriers that you have overcome to create a safe working environment.

Culture

The first and most important barrier to overcome is correct cultural priorities with both leadership and floor employees. This can be difficult to do because safety is not typically on peoples' minds as they work through the rest of their tasks for the day **unless it is a habit and a priority**. Habits are created through repetition and communication. It is management's (i.e. your) responsibility to consistently communicate that a safe environment and behaviors come first, and that it is management's job to remove barriers to that safe environment.

This is compounded by the fact that doing things safely often **does** mean doing them more slowly or deliberately. For example, getting employees to use stools or reaching aids to get hard-to-reach product is slower than having the employee jump for or reach for product. Getting a ladder to open a railcar is slower than straddling a gap between the dock and the car door. Taking one stair at a time on a staircase is slower than taking them two-at-a-time. This fact is not lost on employees in an environment where their jobs depend on being productive. Safety behaviors that are boring, slow, and don't seem to mitigate serious hazards are difficult for employees to follow - they just don't seem important.

How can you change that?

Be "That Guy"

What this means is that you must be a True Believer and leader in your safety program and what it means. You must be at the forefront of safety initiatives, because if you don't live it, no one else will either.

How do you communicate it? A common saying is "slow is smooth, and smooth is fast." This is an effective theme in communicating that following safety procedures will eventually result in high productivity. Remind the team that jumping to tip a box off a high pallet is quicker, but a trip to the hospital to fix the concussion from slipping on the way down is not. Climbing on a rack may help get a pick, but getting fingers caught and broken in the racking decking doesn't help anyone.

Then you must back it up with actions - when an employee brings up productivity concerns because he is doing the right thing for safety, how will you handle it? Do you look away when someone is doing something unsafe that makes your productivity numbers look better? It is very easy to ignore something that is marginally unsafe when it's been done for a while and when everybody else is ignoring it. You must be the leader who notices issues, refuses to accept them, addresses them, and encourages others to do the same.

As an example, I saw employees riding pallets up on forklifts without harnesses to remove high-stacked product along the walls in railcars. It was a very quick but a very unsafe practice. Employees were unsecured on an uneven surface while elevating and moving heavy boxes; it was a recipe for disaster.

In the absence of coherent safety priorities, productivity had taken priority and no one addressed the method of unloading. To address the productivity concern, we changed the unloading process and gave instruction about how and when boxes were supposed to be downstacked during the railcar unload. Without seeing a cubed-out railcar this will be hard to envision, but the change in process allowed team members to have an adequately elevated and stable surface to downstack the boxes. As a result, we ended up with safer working conditions, fewer instances of collapsing walls of boxes, and - incidentally - a more even flow of product to our dock.

Hazard Elimination AND Risk Management

Sometimes the practices or standards that are put into place are indeed stupid overreactions to individuals' carelessness. Some environments can have unreasonable expectations. The purpose of a safety program is to eliminate, reduce, and manage the risks inherent in conducting the business. Taken to its extreme, the only way to completely prevent injuries and incidents is to have all the employees stay home. This is obviously ridiculous, but while it's your responsibility to identify and manage risks, sometimes there are unavoidable accidents (although fewer than most people think). The hard part - which you do during investigations and safety walks - is to identify all the manageable risks and act accordingly.

Culture is driven by **you**, the supervisor, first. You need to be out on the floor and actively viewing your work environment through a Safety lens - looking for hazards, coaching employees, and being an active voice and example for safety. Without that, your team will not take the correct cues on how to behave.

Hazard Recognition

One of the most difficult parts of a good safety culture is getting everyone to always wear their "safety goggles" and recognize hazards. You eventually want everyone to see hazards **before** doing something, not **after** an incident. This comes from communicating about safety every day at every opportunity.

See that pallet on the floor, out of location? That's a trip hazard. Was the pallet in the rack leaning? That's a safety hazard. Were employees following too closely behind each other on their pallet jacks, and not entirely stopping at intersections? Was the proper equipment for a job missing or broken? Were conveyor gates not properly marked? To the safety-aware, those are hazards. To the safety-ignorant, that's getting the work done more quickly, or just business-as-usual.

The point is not that employees should be afraid to leave their homes to come to the site. The point is to sensitize them to potential safety problems before the incidents happen. You will always have risks to manage, but those are much easier to deal with when your team is pointing them out and avoiding them.

Incentives

The second barrier to a healthy safety culture is improper incentives. Improper incentives influence people to make incorrect decisions about safety. Incentives are a part of the culture but are separate from perceptions of safety on the floor.

Look at the motivations of the employees. Employees are frequently reviewed, promoted, moved, or fired based on productivity. Yet there are not very many good ways to tie reviews, promotions, and pay to safety outcomes without creating incentives for under-reporting. The employee's safety participation is judged by the absence of incidents, or on positive management observations, both of which the employee has some but not absolute control over.

In contrast, productivity and quality are highly visible and measurable metrics that the employee has direct control over.

This means that setting the correct safety incentives is very important. These incentives can take two forms: correctives and positive incentives.

Corrective incentives will be most effective in ensuring that employees comply with the letter of the policy, but they do not create a positive safety environment. The employees will act to avoid punishment instead of to be safe. A corrective-driven environment needs to be leavened with much communication about how the changes will prevent injuries or incidents. This communication can be effectively driven on the floor by you, the supervisor, by understanding and talking about why policies are in place. Citing example of incidents related to the policy will help the employees understand why it was put into place.

A "positive" incentive may be a reward or recognition for having a safe environment. The emerging consensus is that offering rewards based on low incident rates incentivizes under-reporting of near-misses and other non-major incidents, robbing the organization of the opportunity to identify and take actions on unsafe conditions. So any rewards or incidents should be based on other safety indicators. I have seen building safety scored on observations of key safety behaviors, which seems like a reasonable substitute, but depends on identifying the right behaviors to score. Other positive incentives include public recognition for engaging in the correct behaviors and for doing positive coaching on a peer level.

When an employee is faced with the choice of being safe or productive, at the margin, what will your employees do? What have you been reinforcing with them that will influence their decisions?

Sustainment

The third barrier to a good safety culture is lack of sustainment mechanisms. A sustainment mechanism is any recurring, documented practice or procedure that causes safety behaviors or awareness to become elevated on employees' daily priorities. Examples of these might include: the active participation and support of a safety committee, regular safety audits, regular safety stand-downs, including Safety notes in the daily start-ups, and safety recognition programs. There are many ways to sustain safety. They vary in form but all of them depend on habit and participation at the supervisor level, so expect to be active in safety activities of various sorts.

The Safety Manager

The safety manager's role is to administer the safety program in the building. Frequently this means managing parts of the culture, conducting audits, and assessing safety impacts of operations. His job is to help you manage risks; he is (or should be) an asset in creating a safe environment, so part of putting changes into place is consulting with him to anticipate any undesired effects.

Some safety managers are very zealous about what you should or shouldn't do according to OSHA and company policies, which can sometimes result in a lot of red tape to get through in order to effect a change. The important thing to remember is that the safety program is there to support Operations and manage risks, not prevent progress.

Actions:

- Look at the online applicable OSHA regulations for your environment; read them, assess your workplace, and recommend or implement changes to be compliant.

- Understand the OSHA definitions of Incident, Incident Rate, Actions, Behaviors, Conditions, and the Hierarchy of Controls.

- Meet your Safety Manager and partner with him on process changes or hazard management.

- During investigations, conduct thorough fact-finding, re-enact the accident with the employees, and include detailed reporting.

- Start Safety Walks or Safety Audits with your employees.

- Recognize employees daily whenever you see safe actions.

- Know your Safety Committee members and involve them in delivering safety messages to the shift.

- Communicate safety reports in start-ups about previous incidents and talk about why new policies or procedures are in place.

- Be the example and enforce safety policies.

Quality

Quality is probably the most difficult concept in warehousing to grasp and communicate. I think of it as "process and output fidelity." That's not a convenient definition, so in other words, quality is the extent to which the process output matches what you want it to output. This means that you must understand the process inputs before you can assess the outputs. It also means you must recognize when your process has poor outputs.

If you're talking to employees, quality is usually synonymous with high accuracy and low damage. Other terms for this include OS&D (Over/Short & Damage) rates, and On-Time-And-In-Full rates, and "shrink." Most of these are measured as rates in percentages or other ratios (like DPMO, or Defects per Million Opportunities). Other measures include your business's measures of quality or accuracy. I worked in a warehouse where the standard was having the pallet racked 2 inches from the upright; that was an indicator of quality. Pick shorts and audits of all kinds give quality measures. As a quality manager, I also closely monitored inventory accuracy metrics. If you can't find it, you can't ship it, so inventory accuracy is an extremely important measure of quality.

Quality Affects Customers

Quality is unique because it directly impacts customer experience. Safety does not directly impact customer experience. Productivity inefficiencies can be covered up with more labor. Quality problems are something that will cause the customer to write about the problem to the CEO and then take his business elsewhere. Additionally, quality issues within a facility have a multiplier effect. The more quality problems you have, the more time that you (or someone else) has to spend fixing those problems before you can put a good product out the door. Rework is a huge cost and pain-in-the-neck that is not readily apparent from looking just at productivity figures.

Quality Inputs

Quality has a lot of factors including process characteristics, tool capabilities, product characteristics, and behavioral inputs.

Some examples of process characteristics include the order in which you train employees to conduct a task, and the thoroughness of exception-handling instructions. Failing to anticipate all the exceptions will inevitably lead to someone discovering the exceptions and devising a creative solution to accomplish the task. Even well-intentioned creativity in a warehouse environment can lead to lost, misplaced, or damaged product. Irritatingly large amounts of time will be spent fixing those exceptions. As a supervisor your role is to know your process capabilities so you can gauge whether the process is being completed correctly.

Tool capabilities also bound what your process can handle. If your RF guns cannot scan beyond a certain distance, or the IT systems are not configured to accept a certain product, or if the rack labels are worn, or if employees have to transmit information by paper instead of RF-system tracking, then you will end up with quality errors that are not always controllable by the employee. If your machines have a certain set of tolerances, and those tolerances can "swiss-cheese" to arrive at a low-quality product, then you must monitor, test, audit, and control for that. As a supervisor, identifying tools and tool deficiencies will require your attention on the floor.

Product characteristics can require your attention to fix or remove. If the product is usually consistent or homogeneous, this is less of a concern than if you are dealing with perishable, delicate, or variable product - think toilet paper or tires versus apples. Fragile or variable product requires more attention to your process to keep quality up.

Behaviors also influence quality because human inputs are variable, leading to variable results. Variability increases quality risk. For example, requiring people to label boxes can result in more mis-positioned labels, incorrect labels, and unreadable labels than if you used machine-applied labels. Even loading a truck requires many behaviorally-controlled quality factors, like where exactly in the truck the pallets are, or how the 'wall' of packages is built. Your people will influence those outputs, so you need to influence them.

So how can you maintain high quality? There are some concepts and tools you can apply to ensure that your team has high quality output.

Measure Quality

What is quality, and what does it mean in your context? If you don't have a quality output measure, start looking for ways. Data can come from over/short reports, pick shorts, cycle counts, misreceives, or process audits. Any time something is wrong, that's a quality error. Count them over time by error type, and you will have quality-data. This will illustrate where the problems are, even if you don't have an immediate solution.

The idea is to gather some sort of feedback on what is causing problems and track it over time. You can do this on a pad of paper, or in an Excel sheet, or on your company's systems.

But if you can't see it and you don't measure it, you can't fix it.

Culture

As with Safety, your team will pick up on your priorities by the frequency and intensity of your communication. Constant communication about the importance of quality work to them - and its effect on the customer - will build awareness. This can be reinforced by publicly recognizing high-quality work, posting quality metrics and numbers, and following up with employees who have quality errors.

Accountability: After identifying and measuring quality, follow up with employees who are creating defects. This ensures that they know of and can correct the errors. This is another aspect of the culture point above. Employees need to know that they are creating defects before they can correct the defects. It's also important to publicly recognize those who have high quality.

Unfortunately, emplacing accountability mechanisms for quality is difficult because the data are sometimes unclear, but regular follow-up for known errors is a good place to start. Defect rates are a fair way to address errors (e.g. having an allowable error percentage for a given task) and having specific known defect types is another. If you do not have accountability for quality issues, you cannot effectively manage productivity. The incentive to produce will overwhelm the incentive to maintain high quality, and you will see multiple errors.

Work as One-Piece Flow: Ensure your employees do one piece of work at a time. Trying to handle multiple tasks or batching tasks will inevitably lead to mis-counted items, lost tags, forgotten product, or other issues. This is the **single biggest process concept** to impress on your team. An employee who is doing picks and scans his pallets ahead of moving them will inevitably result in problems like miscounted products or physical/virtual mismatches, where the employee moves something virtually but not physically. Reconciling these problems is a constant struggle, so you want to prevent as many issues as possible by ensuring your team understands and buys into the importance of doing one thing at a time. There are some environments where batching is used, but that is a deliberate process choice dictated by equipment and other capabilities. Individual employees should not violate the process because it seems quicker to them.

Follow the process: Ensure the employees are following a documented process for accomplishing a task. Many organizations have written processes; read and understand them, so you can understand what your employees are, or are not, doing. If your employees are doing something in different ways, you won't be able to identify where any quality problems are happening. Also, if your employees are not following the written process, any larger process improvement initiatives will be working from bad data for the current state.

Know who owns the process: Identify the gatekeeper of the process. Usually someone owns and controls a given process at a facility or company level. Usually they are the people who are specifically tasked with being subject-matter experts about that process. Knowing those people helps you understand why the process is the way it is and gives you a way to influence future developments in that area.

Actions:

- Read your key process documents. Refresh periodically. Participate in the process periodically to understand what's happening.
- Understand your local quality metrics and standards
- Post Accuracy Rates if available
- Post or read customer feedback at start-ups.
- Ask for quality tips at start-ups.
- Use one-piece flow for all process work.
- Follow up with employees so that they - and you! - understand the errors
- Recognize employees who have consistent high-quality work

Productivity

Productivity is the third of the Big Three and is the most highly visible metric to management because it ties directly into cost, and controlling cost is how the company makes money.

It can't be implemented successfully without Safety and Quality unless you want to take the tradeoffs that it implies, which are an unsafe work environment and poor customer service.

Throughput or Production

Productivity is commonly measured in rates of "things per hour," where those things might be cases received, pallets picked, trucks shipped, bins counted, etc. "Things"" are important because those are the units you can measure. "Per Hour" is important because employees are typically paid on an hourly basis, and efficiency increases are gauged by looking at the ""things per hour" number that the process yields. It's a way to assign cost to production and is easily grasped by employees.

The total amount of production is frequently referred to as *"production"*, *"Throughput"* (TPT), or *"Delivery"* and is calculated in a production environment as:

$$TPT = R * T$$

Where throughput equals the overall hourly production rate (R) multiplied by the number of hours of production (time, T). Delivery and Production are referred to on a daily or weekly or monthly basis, and throughput might be on smaller time intervals.

On a basic level, you need to understand what your planned output is, how many people you have, and what their expected rates are. If you have those pieces of information, you can project how much work you will accomplish in a given number of hours.

In cases where you have multiple sequential processes, you can apply this formula to the sequence to match labor and identify bottlenecks, as shown below.

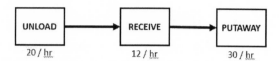

In the diagram, Unloading has a higher rate than Receiving, and both of them have a lower rate than Putaway. If you know that you have 900 items to process, then you need:

Unloading: 900 (items)/ 20 (items/hr) = 45 man-hours
Receiving: 900 (items) / 12 (items/hr) = 75 man-hours
Putaway: 900 (items) / 30 (items/hr) = 30 man-hours

So with a 10-hour shift, you'd need 4.5 FTEs (Full-Time Equivalent) in unloading, 7.5 FTEs in Receiving, and 3 FTEs in Putaway, or 15 FTEs total. If you staff differently, you will end up with bottlenecks or idle labor, and an overall less efficient operation.

We'll look at more applications of this in Production and Staffing.

Rates and Efficiencies

Productivity metrics are also known as efficiencies, which can be ambiguous because efficiency is an abstract noun and not a concrete thing. Regardless, people look at "efficiencies" or efficiency metrics as indicators of how well the business is doing. They will be your primary sets of numbers to monitor. Typically, higher numbers are better, and lower numbers mean you are getting less "bang for the buck" of labor that you're spending.

If you are working in a process, and you don't know or have a firm grasp on the "things per hour" that you do, then you probably want to take a look and see what metrics make sense for that process. These are not always obvious, or the data may not be readily available. Many mature companies utilize WMS systems that can report on productivity or number of transactions of a given type.

For example, I worked in a position as a warehousing supervisor where every night I had a certain number of high-velocity items that needed to get picked for shipping. When I did my staffing rosters, I would allocate headcount by dividing the number of required picks by the rate that I knew those employees would pick at. I'd do the same process concurrently for other things that I had to do.

In another case, I had to look at how long it took to unload and receive a set of railcars. By averaging out the number of pallet-receives that the team could do per direct hour over a shift or working hour, I could solve for how many people I needed to work on unloading those cars to hit a time goal.

This is an optimization problem. Experience and judgment help, but math will help more.

Production Bridges

At some point, you'll be asked why you didn't hit a target production goal or efficiency rate. After all, things are rarely perfect in the warehouse. To help communicate what's going on during the shift, it's worth remembering that process performance is also governed by the Throughput equation. Any negative impacts on your productivity reduce your Rate per hour and will reduce your throughput. Calculating these impacts out is known as bridging the goals; if there are multiple causes, then you have multiple bridges.

For example, say you have a goal of receiving 10,000 units on a shift. Ordinarily, your team receives 1000 units per hour, so you can do the job in a 10-hour shift. However, today the Warehouse Management System went down for 90 minutes. Doing your math with your known rate, you can tell that the impact of the system outage was:

1.5 hours x 1000 units per hour = 1500 units impact

So you should still be able to receive 8500 units, and then effectively communicate the production gap, the cause, and the outcome to the management team.

Applying this logic to any set of efficiencies will help you understand your business and plan realistically. If your putaway process has an engineered standard of 50 units per hour (UPH), but your putaway location occupancy is at 98% full, and you know that efficiency declines by 3% for every 1% incremental occupancy over 90% full, then your expected rate after the efficiency impact would be:

$$50UPH - 50\ UPH * [3\% * (98 - 90)] = 38UPH$$

With 38 UPH as your new impacted rate, you can calculate what your production for the shift will be. And you'll be able to plan, understand what your barriers are, and communicate why your production has been affected.

Direct vs Indirect Labor

Direct labor hours are the hours spent by the people actually doing the thing that makes money for the company. Indirect hours are spent completing tasks that don't directly contribute to "things per hour", but that still have to be done. Examples include cleaning, running pallets, doing inventory control tasks, problem-solving, or processing damaged items.

Larger companies will likely already have defined productivity metrics in place, or rates.

Indirect roles rarely have rates because their workflows are either not measurable or discrete. You need to be aware of how many indirect hours you are spending, because those roles are not as accessible to oversight as direct roles are, and it is very easy to overstaff on indirect hours without objective staffing guidelines.

Indirect labor is also measured in rates of "things per hour", but those rates are mostly abstractions designed to help measure the "spread" of indirect hours over the actual work. They will tell you if you are spending too many indirect hours for the work you're doing, or - interestingly - can indicate that you're spending too *few* hours on completing essential upkeep tasks. The key here is to monitor your indirect rates (e.g., indirect hours per units processed) and have a target rate so you can develop and tell on a given day whether you were over- or under-spending.

For example, warehouse operators can be assigned as "runners" who move product between a dock and a putaway location. They may not have to scan the product - their job is strictly to move product off the dock. One way to develop a target rate would be to measure receiving volumes and hours required to move the product off the dock, and then apply that ratio in your staffing before you start each day. If on average you have 600 pallets to move in a day, and require 30 hours to move them, then your ratio is 20 pallets/hr. If your projected workload is 500 pallets, then similarly to direct labor rates, you would need to staff 25 hours on the dock.

Influencing Productivity

You can influence productivity through staffing, performance management, and changing the actual processes themselves.

Staffing, as mentioned in the "Operations" section, should be allocated to your work. If you find that you have excess hours in your department for a shift, then let your manager or peers know so you can get the right amount of people to the right workload. This is directly and mathematically tied to how productive your shift is.

Performance management is the carrots and the sticks of keeping people motivated. It is being able to hold people accountable to standards of performance (like the rates mentioned earlier) as well as giving positive recognition to the members of your team who exceed the standard. If you don't effectively manage performance, your team will not be productive. It may then develop a culture of low performance which will be difficult to change.

Changing the actual processes is a larger project but has high impacts over the long term. At a local level, on the shift, you may have limited options when it comes to changing an actual core process, but you may have great latitude in how you accomplish locally controlled processes.

Companies like to have standard processes so they can get reliable information on how a given process is currently working. If the processes are not standard from building to building or even shift to shift, it is very difficult to tell what works and what doesn't on a large scale. Further, process changes can have upstream or downstream effects that you're not aware of. What looks like a simple change to you could have quality effects downstream that you don't see and aren't aware that you're creating. This is why you should coordinate process changes with your boss and any directly affected departments before implementing.

That said, it's well worth asking "why" a process is done in a particular way. There may be very quick, easy, and locally controllable changes that you can implement. It's one thing if you are recommending that the picking process be re-configured in the WMS, which would require large-scale testing and implementation. It's another if you've figured out that you can get your startups done more efficiently by changing the parking configuration of the PIT in your area or giving instructions on how to do something within the scope of the current process.

You should let your boss know the opportunities that you see, but coordinate changes ahead of time.

Actions

- Identify your key production processes

- Identify your key indirect processes

- Understand your rates - where to find your "Things-Per-Hour" and "TPH" goals for direct and indirect processes

- Understand rate expectations for your employees and find out how they were derived

- Identify where to find production records by employee over a given time

- Identify the workload for the shift

- Check - are you staffing to the work? Are you performance-managing your team? Is there a management process at your site for performance?

- Look for improvement opportunities in the process

- Recognize your productive employees

- Coach the employees who need help

Processes

Before we go on, throughout this handbook I mention "process" as though it's some sort of mystical thing, e.g. "Try to improve the process."

Some organizations treat process as a sacred goal to be achieved, like a higher state of enlightenment. You'll hear "Follow the process," as though the Process is the Gospel.

There is some truth in this. You do need to look at most aspects of your operation through a "process lens."

A process is an orderly series of actions or steps taken to achieve a goal. Many companies have documented, reproducible processes. This helps you, the supervisor, a lot: you have the path blazed for you on how to do things. Refer to the process documents that your company has, and keep in mind that these processes can be in just about any function - HR, Floor operations like Shipping and Receiving, Safety, and so on. Methods of controlling process can include any known sequence of events, like having checklists, calendar invites, audit plans, et cetera.

Further, processes extend beyond just the documented way to use an RF gun to pick cases. Processes also encompass how people communicate and interact. Regular meetings are a type of process. Running a shift is a process. Stand-up meetings are a process within the process of running a shift. Sending emails to get something done can be a process, if it recurs. Sometimes the process is tightly defined, and sometimes it is very loosely organized.

Your goal, when you see a mess of activity going on, or a lot of product piled up in one location, is to determine what outcome you're looking for, and what process applies. It is important to think about how you operate in terms of process. If you don't think that way at least a little bit, you will never know what to expect, and won't be able to quickly identify when things are out of specification.

Before you start thinking about implementing safety, quality, or productivity improvements, first understand the process that is currently going on. If you are not clear on what to do, and you know that the activity will repeat or that the outcome will have to happen again, look for the process.

Standard Work

Standard work is the cornerstone of consistent process. Standard work is defined as a set of steps to accomplish a process in a given cycle time, takt[1] time, and with a certain amount of Standard Work in Process (SWIP). The steps are usually engineered to balance flow through a process and are often documented in detail.

That part of the setup is usually not a supervisor's responsibility; the supervisor is responsible for ensuring any sort of standard work instructions are followed throughout the department's processes. If your facility or business has documented standard work, familiarize yourself with it so that you can assess how well your team is following it, and how to educate them on what they need to do.

Auditing

Auditing is checking key process inputs and outputs. You can do this with any sort of indicators - floor presence will indicate whether the flow is being followed; spot-checking your team members' work will determine whether the standard work is being followed; reports will show at a high level whether you are achieving the process results that you're looking for. As a supervisor, an important part of your role is to audit your key processes often during your shift to identify problems or pain-points for your team.

As an example, checking production after the first hour is a form of auditing the process as well as individual performance. Walking the floor will give you visual feedback on any process

---

[1] *"Takt time"* is a Lean term derived from the German term "Taktzeit", referring to cycle time. It is the interval of customer demand on a process. It can be calculated by dividing the time available to work per period by the customer demand per period.

breakdowns because you will see something that is out of place or out of balance.

Further, you don't necessarily have to complete all audits. You can assign your team members to complete some of these for you - a standard process audit can be as simple as having your leads count the number of pallets remaining on the dock at the end of a shift, and reporting it in an end-of-shift report. This sort of activity will give you quantifiable data that you can look at over time to see if the process is being followed and if it is improving over time.

Exceptions

Although processes are not perfectly set in stone, they are the default expectation that everyone expects that you will follow. If you are going to go outside of a process, ensure that you are doing it deliberately, for a reason, and that you inform anyone who is affected by the change that there is a change. 'Over-communicate' the change in the situation so that it is painfully obvious to everyone involved.

This is because you create exceptions when you go outside of a process. Organizations that are used to doing things a certain way are often bad at handling exceptions. Exceptions require extra communication to handle. They are typically undocumented. Because they are not within the boundaries of the normal process, they have the potential to create unanticipated errors and problems.

Here are two examples:

My company's sales team had a request for a special type of product handling involving securing the product with a special type of packaging on a truck. The ordinary way to communicate the change was to put the handling request into the system notes associated with that customer. However, Sales had circulated the request only by email to a few people and expected the Shipping department to follow up on it. Because the instructions weren't accessible in the usual place, the loaders didn't know to follow the instructions. As you'd expect, some loads were shipped incorrectly. Afterward, we identified that the usual process for inputting instructions hadn't been followed, and as a result the customer was disappointed.

Another time, some special handling for an Xbox sales event was requested. The product manager made sure to communicate explicitly about what had to happen to the product handling and putaway in order to get the right Xboxes out the door on time. Although the handling was highly irregular, several meetings supported with email correspondence to the people directly involved ensured that everyone was informed and on the same page, so the project was completed without incident.

You will run into "special" situations or requests. One of the first things you should do is ask whether there is a process for what you're doing. If there's not, then you will want to over-communicate about what's going on and consider putting a process together to handle the exception in the future.

Identifying Process Barriers

As a supervisor, you should be able to identify when and where process barriers are occurring.

First, if you are not getting your expected outputs, then there is a problem. Outputs can include productivity output or quality output. For productivity, if the process is not producing what it is supposed to when it is supposed to, then there is a problem or barrier. If you are seeing more defects or errors than usual, then there is a problem.

Additionally, a build-up of *anything* is a problem because it indicates a bottleneck somewhere in your processes. It shows that process capabilities are not matched. If you see a pile of product waiting to be handled, there is a barrier. A crowd of people waiting for something indicates a barrier.

Implied here is that you need to know what your expected outputs are in the first place, and what "normal" looks like. Without knowing those things, you will not be able to identify problems in your operation.

There is a wide variety of literature on identifying and fixing process problems. Some references are listed in "Resources."

A Very Quick Primer On How To Identify Waste

Many process barriers are self-inflicted and fall under the category of "waste." Waste is just what it sounds like - extra and unnecessary time, effort, or material spent doing something. Lean process methodology typically identifies seven basic types of waste:

1) Overproduction - making too much of something. Often identified by "too much stuff" in an area where it shouldn't be; hearing "we need space" is a red flag for this waste. This is the first and highest-impact of all the wastes.

2) Inventory - tying money, space, and material up in holding product

3) Transportation - moving things around unnecessarily (for example, moving product around multiple times en route to the final destination)

4) Motion - extra, unneeded movement, often from poor process layouts, inconveniently located tools, or even poor IT tools that cause long research times. This can cause wear and tear on people and equipment.

5) Over-processing - Rework and handling beyond what the customer needs to get the job done

6) Waiting - idle time, usually at a bottleneck, when something else isn't ready to work on. Do your people have to wait on something to do their jobs? That's waste.

7) Defects - When the job isn't done right the first time, someone has to correct it, and the time and effort and material from the first go-round is wasted.

There is extensive literature on Lean wastes and how to address them, so this is purely introductory. But these are the areas to look at for improving your processes. Does your team have to travel long distances when they could be traveling short distances? Are your pallet-jack operators "back-hauling" product or material on their trips through the warehouse? Is the team creating poor products that have to be fixed later or reworked? Is there simply too much "stuff" being produced, that must be handled, moved, and transported throughout the warehouse? Are there bottlenecks in your processes that are causing your team to wait idly?

Any of these things happening are opportunities for improvement. Knowing these types of waste will help you identify those opportunities when you see them.

Some people add an eighth waste "Human potential," but that is just making explicit the opportunity costs incurred by the above. You can't get the most out of people when you are wasting their time and efforts.

Barriers

Barriers to your team's success can come in many shapes and flavors. Part of your job as a supervisor is to remove those barriers so they can do their jobs. Those barriers may include:

- Equipment that doesn't work (including IT problems, broken PIT, printers, RF guns, poor user interface, etc)
- Lack of supplies and equipment
- Processes that are inherently wasteful or undependable
- Lack of expectations
- Having the wrong people on the team
- Poor HR support infrastructure

Or any of many things that keep your team from doing a good job. An initial reaction to some of these things may be "Hey, you've got to just deal with it." But it's important for you, the supervisor, to recognize that these are not examples of your people being ignorant or incompetent. These are things keeping your people from getting their work done.

Equipment That Doesn't Work

I found that sometimes team members would complain about some pieces of equipment operating more slowly than others, and they would go for the "good" equipment as soon as possible. In other places I've heard about RF scanners not operating properly, dropping reception, and so forth. A common reaction of leadership is to check the equipment and shrug, because either the problem or solution is not immediately apparent and, anyway, hey, it's kind of working, right?

This indifference to the issues represents an ignorance of the very real barriers to performance that the team is facing. Anyone who has ever struggled to get an RF scanner working understands this frustration. It's very real when that scanner is standing between you and being productive, and productivity is how you keep your job.

Further, when the reporting is twice-removed from the problem (e.g. if the team member has to report to a supervisor, who then reports to a manager or to IT to solve) then the real knowledge of the problem is lost, and the person who might be able to solve it doesn't have the information they need to fix the issue.

The solution is to thoroughly and personally understand the problem, and then get in touch with the support needed to fix it. Or put the person with the problem in touch with the support. Anything less risks leaving the problems unfixed, which simultaneously reduces productivity and undermines your credibility with your team.

Lack of Supplies and Equipment

Hoarding is a phenomenon resulting from the fact that, contrary to some perceptions, most people want to do their jobs, and to do them well. If adequate equipment is not available to do those jobs, then some employees will hoard and hide equipment. This results in more shortages for everyone. Then more people start hiding equipment. The situation spirals.

This is what happens in an environment with market shortages - the perception of shortage quickly becomes reality. Where you might have only been one radio short yesterday, but today you are missing four radios because employees have hidden them so that they are available for work on the next shift.

To combat this, you need two things:
1) Adequate equipment, or
2) Clearly designated roles who get the equipment, and
3) Accountability for your equipment and supplies

At a Railex facility, we noticed that we had difficulty keeping the docks clean. Brooms and shovels had designated locations, but often couldn't be found. Talking to the team indicated that people were "hiding" the supplies so they knew that they would always be available. We went out and bought supplies for most of the locations in the building to address the perception of scarcity, and suddenly people stopped hiding supplies. Perception management can be very important for even very simple things like brooms, and even more so for other more expensive equipment.

Accountability can mean any process to ensure that you keep all of your equipment. I have seen sign-out processes, physical security measures, and a couple other solutions. This is difficult, even within the warehouse, if you have any shortages at a moment between departments whether due to repairs or actual shortages. Even within the warehouse, you may have trouble keeping track of where your equipment is, but if you do not do it then you will lose it. I recommend between-shift audits of equipment and assigning equipment by department to ensure that clear visibility on the equipment exists.

Bad Process

A bad process is any set of steps or instructions that doesn't support what your team is doing. This can happen in several ways, but the most clear articulation of it is thinking - again- in terms of the seven forms of waste (*muda*, in Lean-speak):

- Overproduction
- Inventory
- Motion
- Transportation
- Over-processing
- Waiting
- Defects

Detail on each of these forms of waste and how to recognize them is available in Lean methodology literature, but for our purposes anything that causes your team to do extra of any of these things is a bad process. Do they have to move around more than needed? Does the process create (or make it likely to create) mistakes and defects? Is there a big pile of "stuff" somewhere? Are your team members waiting around to do work? These things are signals of barriers to optimal production. The rule of thumb is that if it looks wasteful or wrong, it probably is.

Bad processes are bad for another reason: Your employees know they are bad. They may not be able to articulate exactly why the processes suck, but they do know that they get frustrated, that the work is difficult to get right, and that things just *seem* harder than they have to be. There are few things more demoralizing than wanting to do a good job, being hampered by your environment or conditions, and then having no one understand what's causing the problems. Holding someone accountable for the results of a poor process is a good way to frustrate your team.

Lack of Expectations

If your employees do not have a **very** clear conception of what is expected of them, they will not be able to meet those expectations. If they're not able to meet the expectations because they don't know the expectations, then you have failed as a supervisor. This is to say that you should be consistently and often communicating standards, whether for safety, production, quality, or general behaviors. Providing feedback on expectations can be difficult, but it's easy to do en masse and before you have to let someone know that he isn't meeting them.

To do this, **you** need to understand the expectations. If they are unclear to you, ask your manager what the standard is and what right looks like, and **why** the standards are that way. This will help you understand what the intent of the standards is, so you can make better judgment calls and give guidance to your team as necessary.

For example, a standard at Amazon was that every item being put away had to be scanned with the RF gun. This was definitely slower than visually counting and manually typing the count of the items to be put away into the scanner. However, the reasoning was that manually inputting numbers increased the probability of typos on the scanner or other inaccuracies. Since every error required at least two more visits to the location to verify the inventory, the tradeoff of being a bit more accurate was worth being a bit slower on the initial putaway. A supervisor who did not understand why the team was being asked to do something more slowly would be unable to explain to his team why the slower process was better than the faster one, and in a production environment this would have prevented buy-in from the team.

Having the Wrong People

Sometimes, and although everyone has his own strengths and weaknesses, you will simply have the wrong people on the team. The remedy for this may be to coach those people so that they perform correctly and fit well with everyone else, but that may also not be possible for reasons that are out of your control.

When you identify this, then it is your responsibility to move those people off the team. They may fit better on another team in the business, so long as you're not exporting problems somewhere else. If they are behavioral or performance problems, then you need to clearly understand that and take appropriate action to work them out of the organization. At that point you should partner with HR to develop the proper next steps to move them out.

As an example, I had an associate who did not function well on the team. She met performance goals but would frequently take breaks to socialize during production hours. This caused a lot of discontent in the rest of the team. Further, she tried to mask her non-working time and socializing by being logged into her RF scanner, so it didn't look to the casual observer as though she was doing anything wrong. She was very resistant to feedback on her behaviors. After getting several peer reports, I determined that this was a problem and began issuing corrective actions with HR's buy-in on the behaviors. She did not self-correct and we let her go. Other individuals who were influenced by her negative attitude returned their focus to the job at hand, and I received discrete thanks from several team members for working through that issue.

Poor HR Support Infrastructure

Your employees are people. While this can be surprising to many supervisors, it is a fact. The corollary is that those people have people issues, from personal lives to benefit management. A strong HR support presence will make your job easier by communicating consistent policies for how to deal with situations. However, if you do not have much HR support in place, then you will find it difficult to manage your team. You will need closer coordination with your manager for more situations, including the benefit management, performance management progressions, and numerous other situations that will come up.

If your HR department is weak or policies are inconsistent, then you will spend more time on those issues than you would otherwise have to, and this becomes a barrier to good performance on the floor. To combat this, seek clarifications for issues ahead of time, ask about exceptions to rules, and escalate decisions that you are not sure about.

Running the Shift

The shift is the basic unit of supervisor work.

How to Organize A Shift

The supervisor's job is to run a shift. It's important to recognize that shift work in distribution is a process, and the goal is that the hourly employees have boring, repetitious days. In many cases, the days will have special requirements to accomplish, but that should ideally not affect the hourly employees.

Shifts have five parts:

- Prep

- Start-up

- Production

- End-of-shift & handoff

- Post-shift

These components can and should be divided further for preparatory purposes. It's important to realize that each of these parts are not entirely smooth-flowing, and that the transition points between them represent seams in the daily process – almost as though each is a station on an assembly line. The supervisor's job is to make them flow smoothly with minimal transition time between them.

Prep

Preparation for a shift will set the stage for your success during the shift. Successful preparation can be summarized in the 4M Model – ensuring that you have the Manpower, Methods, Materials, & Machines to be successful. There is also a crucial element of building situational awareness that will help identify issues and goals, avoid problems, and resolve conflicts.

Shift prep should involve:

- Reviewing the production or delivery plan

- Preparing the staffing roster

- Checking call-outs and adjusting the staffing roster

- Walking the floor, with the outgoing supervisor if available

- Ensuring the required supplies or equipment are available for your shift

Reviewing a production plan frequently involves checking the status of any ongoing operations on the company's production tracking system, whether that be online or paper-based. This will scope the amount and type of the work that you have ahead of you for the duration of the shift. Then you can put labor against it on your staffing roster.

This means building the **staffing roster**, which is a list of everyone on your shift and every position or type of work you need to fill. If you don't have an accurate roster then you're going to want one to keep on hand at all times during the shift to make timely decisions and in case of emergencies. Roster preparation should dovetail closely with whatever the plan for the day is so that you can allocate FTEs (Full Time Equivalents) to the work. The next section will cover staffing in more detail.

At this point you should determine whether you are **correctly staffed** to the work. This means checking whether you have too much, too little, or the right amount of labor to accomplish what's in front of you. If you have too much or too little, it's time to check with your peers or manager to see what the options are – whether another department needs the labor, whether you can get help, or whether it's time to send people home with Voluntary Time Off or a Lack-of-Work situation.

The **floor-walk** is a critical part of getting ready for the shift but is often overlooked because it takes time and some activation energy to accomplish. Even though it's easier to sit in the office and do rosters or send emails, take a few minutes – even 2-5 minutes –– to walk the floor, cover as much ground as possible with a notebook, and return to the start-up area.

Being present on the floor will inform you about what work is pending and what still has to be done; where product or material is out of place; the general state of cleanliness; and generally increase situational awareness beyond what comes through emails or conversations. Doing the walk with the previous supervisor helps ensure that critical hand-off items are not missed. It helps build the knowledge to share priorities with the team as well as communicating why (or not) certain things happened.

This is important because a frequent source of friction inside a building is between teams – *"Those Nights guys cherry-picked all the good stuff, and now we're left picking the hard stuff!"*

Or

"Days never cleans up, look at this out-of-place product in the aisle again!"

A good hand-off helps ensure that problems are identified for fixing while the people with the knowledge of what did (or did not) happen are still there. Being able to share "why" something happened will help build credibility with your team and build teamwork across the building.

The final element of prep (although it may take place earlier, depending on your facility and rhythm) is ensuring that **equipment is available** for the incoming shift. This can include ensuring that RF scanners are available, that carts or PIT is plugged in and charging, and generally that your team will be able to get what they need to do work.

After shift prep is the start-up, the actual shift's work (production), and the end-of-shift period where you get ready for the transition to the next shift.

Staffing

Staffing is a critical part of a supervisor's job. It is the process of putting the right amount of labor to tasks and then adjusting labor throughout the shift.

Before the shift, you should understand two things:

1) What your shift's staffing roster contains - what your headcount is, and what positions or functions you need to fill.

2) What your day's workload is. This is sometimes called the production plan or delivery plan.

Within the roster, you will gain familiarity about who is trained in which tasks, and who is good at those tasks. Knowing the strengths and weaknesses of your team members will help you staff effectively in the short- and long-term. But before you get there, you need to know how many people you have and what work you have to do. Then you should know what the expected rates for accomplishing given tasks are. Many workplaces have task standards; some do not, but a few days' observation can quickly inform you.

Determining Process Rates

If your company does not already have rates, then determine the rates for your key processes by taking all the work your employees did over a shift and divide it by the number of hours in the shift.

Rate = Work * Time

That will give you a good base average. Do that for 2-3 days' of data and you will have a fairly reliable sense of what the planning expectations should be.

Applying Rates to Staffing

The next step is to apply the rates to your workload.

For example, if I have:

- 50,000 items to pick for the day, and

- 20 team members initially staffed doing case-pick and

- Each team member can pick 200 cases/hour

- The working shift is 10 hours long

Then at the end of the day, I would have 10 hrs * 200 items/hour * 20 team members = 40,000 cases picked (actually, a bit less because of the start-up meeting and breaks – don't forget to account for those!).

Uh oh! If I want to hit the goal, I'd want to have 50,000 cases picked. This means that at this staffing level I will be behind on my daily goal of 50,000. At this point, I can do the math and figure out that with:

- 10 productive hours in a shift

- 50,000 to pick

- Pick rates of 200/hr

That I need a total of 25 employees ($X = 50,000/(10 * 200)$) in process to accomplish the goal.

Now I can adjust my initial staffing before completing the plan and assess whether I need to coordinate to achieve the goal. After doing this for the rest of my key processes, I can develop a plan to shift labor or go ask other departments for help.

This analysis can be completed in virtually any setting with some amount of work remaining, some amount of time remaining, a good guess on rate expectations, and a pocket calculator or pencil and paper. The rate expectations don't need to be perfect, but you will need a good basic understanding of what to reasonably expect.

The relevant formulas are:

Production = Rate * Time

Overall Rate = # Employees * Production Rate/Hour

Indirect Labor

Not all jobs have rates or even quantifiable output. Problem-solving or damage-rework, for example, is usually not measured on a productivity basis, but it still needs to be staffed. To properly account for these, ensure you designate all jobs on your staffing roster. That way you will assign a name to the job and there will be a specific person designated to accomplish it.

Some of these jobs will require some additional attention. If you put someone on an indirect function, you will need to follow up or give specific instructions on what to do, when to do it, and how long to do it - otherwise, you may end up wasting time on something that's less important than production. If you didn't tell your team member that he was only supposed to work on damage from lunch until the 2nd break, he might end up at the damage area for the whole shift. These jobs require you to keep strong situational awareness of the amount of indirect labor required to run smoothly. Sometimes it is a lot, and sometimes it will not be very much.

Because of this, you may end up double-booking or having to sequence work. Your plan might be to have the team member in production for the first half of the day, and then move to something else. Not everyone has to stay in the same function for the whole shift, and if you plan for expected needs, then you will have to make fewer adjustments later.

Adjusting Staffing

You should monitor production often during the shift to determine whether your team is keeping up to the plan that you originally staffed for. If they are, then you may have the opportunity to get ahead on work or complete other activities. If not, then you will need to adjust staffing to meet your priority goals. I recommend adjusting staffing at roughly the quarter-shift marks. Though this is not hard-and-fast, it prevents yo-yo'ing your employees all over to put out fires. Moving employees around between processes too much will incur switching costs - they have to physically go to another place, sometimes get another piece of equipment, and change processes. This means that they will slow down. When they slow down, you lose additional productivity, and compound the problem you're trying to fix in the first place.

If you move them at natural breaks in the flow of the shift, then the switching costs will already to some extent be built into the shift, and you won't lose as much productivity. Additionally, your employees won't be confused about what they're doing, and you'll have a more predictable plan. The only caveat to this is that limiting when you do moves does limit your flexibility, so you need to make some planning assumptions about what's important and how close you will be to your process goals.

Job Rotation

Not all jobs are equal, and your employees know it. Your employees aren't equal either, and **you** know it. You'll want to staff your strongest people where they will have the most impact, or where you don't want to worry about what's going on.

But don't, or at least not all the time. Plan to rotate your employees through different jobs even if they aren't the strongest. Although this is an unnatural tendency, it will solve a few problems for you:

1) Specialization - you will have more employees who can accomplish more tasks. Experience equals On-the-job cross-training, which will ultimately allow you to be more flexible in your staffing in tight situations or when key people call out or go on vacation.

2) Fairness - maintaining consistent job rotation completely negates charges of unfairness or discrimination that might come up. It's hard to argue that the boss likes Joe more than Bill when they were getting the same job rotation. On the other hand, if Joe always got the sought-after indirect role, then Bill has a stronger case.

The way to accomplish job rotation is to have an ordered list of your employees, and a list of all your staffing positions. As you make up rosters daily, start with the next name on your rotation list and work through each position. This can become complicated if employees have multiple (but not all!) competencies in your department, but if you have a consistent, posted list, as well as communicate in advance what happens in special situations (e.g. when a vacation or personal day disrupts the order), then your team will understand what is happening and why.

Printed Rosters

As you make your roster or assignment sheet, print it out and carry a copy with you during the shift. This will be a helpful reference for knowing where your people are and where they are supposed to be. It serves as a map for adjusting labor during your shift. Also, for safety reasons, if an emergency happens you will need a roster to take accountability of your employees.

An example of an assignment sheet for a small picking shift is below. Note that the date, major functional positions, staff assignments, and blocks to check attendance are included. A document like this is helpful for planning and tracking staffing moves and can be posted so that your team understands their jobs at the start of the day.

Assignment Sheet

Date	

Lead	Catie

Picking			Problem Solving	
Bob			Liz	
Joe			John	
Tina				
Bill				

Pallet Jack			Audits	
Kevin			Kirvi	
Justin			Steve	

A spreadsheet template with your key jobs and cells to fill in with names is the best tool for this. Templates can also be set with rates to instantly calculate and give you a picture of how many pieces of work you can expect to process in the span of a shift with a given staffing list.

Training Rosters

For job rotation and physical rosters, it's helpful to have a list of each employee and what that employee can do in the warehouse. This is not a big deal if you have two positions in the warehouse.

It is a big deal when you are managing 200 employees and interact with four other departments who sometimes need help, or if you have five or 10 different roles within your department that require separate training. A list by name with everyone's trained roles will help you manage those situations effectively and will help you determine who to train on new skills.

Actions:

- Build a roster/assignment sheet with all your employees and functions to fill during a shift

- Staff each position with a name

- Plan to flex labor as needed

- Ensure you are rotating your roster

- Carry the printed roster during shift

The Start-Up

Part of a Process

The start-up itself can vary by operation, but it is a critical part in shift operation - remember, it is part of a process. It frames first-hour productivity and is the vehicle for communicating to your team about staffing plan and workload, safety, quality, building events, and any other items that come up. Some organizations use start-ups to conduct stretching and warm-ups as well to mitigate injuries.

Start-ups should be conducted as close to the work as feasible in a designated area. I've seen start-ups conducted in breakrooms when temperatures or noise wouldn't allow on-the-floor meetings, but ideally the start-up is on the warehouse floor as close to equipment and work as possible. This is to minimize frictional time traveling and to allow the leader to talk more concretely about Operations-related topics.

There should be a clear time standard to have the start-up communication complete and have everyone out on the floor and actively in production. If you're unclear on what that time standard is, ask your manager. A general benchmark is that 7 minutes is adequate to communicate about Safety, staffing, daily assignments, conduct any stretching or other communication, and get people moving to production.

Script It

Communication at start-ups should be somewhat scripted ahead of time to ensure that key communication gets through. Notecards and/or previously-published building-wide notes will ensure that you don't forget critical information. Remember, this is one of only a few times that you get to communicate with your whole team – this will set the tone for what they're thinking of and what they prioritize during the day.

A template for conducting a start-up might include:

1) **Greeting:** "Hey it's good to see everyone, who's ready for another day of box-moving excellence?!" You want to get people engaged and energized and officially start the meeting.

2) **Safety:** Safety tip or message for the day

3) **Recognition**: Take a moment to recognize your team's accomplishments or allow team members to recognize each other.

4) **Quality**: A quality message to ensure that the team is aware of quality issues and things to look for.

5) **Production:** Production plan and staffing for the day. You can cover efficiency numbers and delivery goals here.

6) **Building announcements:** Any messaging that the team needs to hear about other projects, hiring opportunities, upcoming events, etc.

7) **Questions:** Take a few questions from the team.

Having the team members share a safety tip and quality tip can also increase team member engagement in those areas. Having the manager tell the group to do something is one technique; hearing a peer talk about a way to avoid errors brings credibility and relevance to those messages. Taking questions at the end is important because the team members will bring up concerns that you can address to the group, instead of having them ask questions individually, or failing to address problems on your team.

Transition Management

When I was a cadet, I competed in the USMA Sandhurst competition. Sandhurst is a competitive team event through a 7- or 8-mile obstacle course through the April rain-sodden Hudson River Valley mountains while completing skills stations like rappelling, boating, and marksmanship, and over various obstacles like hills, walls, and culverts. Teams were graded on time and points earned, and winners got bragging rights for the next year. Teams would practice together for a semester for all the skills stations and strategize about how to overcome obstacles.

The obvious discriminators between teams were skills proficiency (How fast did you get everyone over that wall?!) and physical conditioning. However, a key—though often-overlooked—component that excellent teams rehearsed was eliminating transition times, or the time between events and moving on the actual course. Even if team members could run fast and shoot well, that didn't mean squat if they couldn't transition smoothly between running and shooting. But since the transition wasn't an obvious event, mediocre teams often neglected practicing the coordination needed to get transitions as close to zero as possible.

In Lean parlance and an operations setting, transition times might be changeover times – *mudas*[2] of waiting or processing.

In a factory, transition times might be obvious - the die has to be changed out or material has to be added to a machine. In a warehouse or operations environment where labor hours mean productivity, the same thing applies but may be less obvious. How does your team handle transition times between tasks?

Start of Shift (SOS) is a key transition time, when everyone is getting in, getting oriented, getting equipped, and getting into process. From the time they clock in to production, they are waiting. This is waste. A 15-minute startup period on an 8-hr shift takes 3% of your productivity off the top – simple math for sure, but you've got to make that up later. It's easy to slip, and before you know it, 20 or 30 minutes have gone by before everyone is operating... and that's a lot of opportunity.

Your team might be great at its core processes, but have you looked at what non-value-added activity happens at SOS? How are you setting them up for success? Are your shift start-up meetings smooth and prepared? Are your team members getting

---

[2] Refer to *The Toyota Way* or books by Shigeo Shingo for further reading on Lean wastes and ways to eliminate them.

what they need – like scanners or instructions - right away? Are you communicating efficiently, and are you thinking two steps ahead to where the team needs to be in 15 minutes?

You can help facilitate that by setting standards for start-ups to ensure consistent results. Some examples might be:

- How long should a start-up take? As mentioned earlier, a clear time standard gives a benchmark for your leadership to plan against for communicating and getting the team into action.

- Ensuring constant roster accuracy can save time and confusion in getting staffing-to-function correct, particularly during a peak holiday season if lots of new faces are around.

- Communication: Safety, building announcements, performance, and daily plans can be prepared ahead of time for a thorough but efficient communication plan, and centrally-coordinated communication (e.g. announcements to read) ensures a consistent message across shifts.

- Equipment should be ready for use – having scanners ready for handing out or picking up, equipment parked in the appropriate location, etc, can save you from having multiple team members standing around without being able to be ready.

This can take another several minutes if not properly planned for by having equipment available. If your team is taking 15 minutes to get into process, including the start-up, then you've already lost 2.5% of available time for production. This is not to minimize the importance of start-up communication, but more to emphasize that a crisp start-up plan should be deliberate and well-executed.

In one position, I found out that shifts were taking upwards of 30 minutes from SOS to get into process on an 11.5-hr shift. That was 4%+ of available time that was being lost simply due to poor execution. This is an easy thing to monitor and influence that can have dramatic results on your ability to execute.

Transitions happen at start-ups, around break times and lunches as employees exit and re-enter their processes, and toward the end-of-shift as they start getting ready to leave work. Be aware of how you are managing these key transition points to avoid having your productive time "leak."

Production

Managing production on a shift is the meat-and-potatoes of a supervisor's job. This is the fun part!

Your shift should be a planned event and have a regular rhythm. If you walk in not knowing how your shift is going to go, then you're not prepared.

Continuous monitoring of production during the shift is required to stay situationally aware of any barriers that the employees might be facing, but there are some checkpoints and processes that you can institute to ensure that you are staying aware.

The first step is setting up a daily standard-work checklist for yourself as a **guideline** – not straitjacket – for checking key actions and metrics during the shift. An example follows:

Standard work example:

Pre-Shift	Start-up	Notes
Check Email	Safety Tip	
Check Call-ins	Quality Tip	
Verify production plan	Recognition	
Prepare staffing roster	Building announcements	
Floor walk	Production Plan	
	Staffing	
	Questions	

1st qtr	2nd qtr	Notes
Start-up	Adjust staffing at break	
Check first-hour productivity	Monitor production	
Send 1st Qtr Update	Check inventory piles	
Deliver outstanding feedback	Check damage & rework areas	
Check first-quarter productivity		

3rd Qtr	4th Qtr	Notes
Adjust staffing at Break	Adjust staffing at break	
Lunch start-up	Check last-hour productivity	
Email mid-shift report	Check damage & rework areas	
Monitor production	Prepare handoff report	

This is a very simple example, but it should be simple enough that it's realistic and reminds you when to do the important things.

Progress in many cases can be monitored continuously, but there are some key points that you should check:

- **First-hour productivity**. This is a function of the execution of the start-up and how quickly the team got into production. A good first hour is a bellwether for the rest of the shift and understanding where improvement in this easy-to-address step is available. You should check your productivity against where you think you should be at the end of your first hour. If you are behind your 1st-hour goal, adjust your staffing or expectations, or otherwise figure out where you fell behind so that you can fix it next time. Communicate your status to your Ops manager. Check with the team to identify barriers.

- **Production Meeting:** Many buildings have production meetings an hour or two after the shift starts to ensure everybody has what they need and is on track for the day. This is an easy way to make sure everyone is on the same page and that any issues are identified and addressed.

- **Quarterly production against goals**. Many organizations have shifts set up to include 2 short breaks as well as a lunch, resulting in a shift being split into four "quarters." These are good opportunities to check progress against overall production goals for the day, identify potential shortfalls, and shift labor around during a natural break in the flow of production. Quarterly checkpoints are also good times to check with and coach any team members having trouble with rates or performance. Shifting labor "mid-stream" **between** breaks results in additional switching time from one process to another that shows as lost productivity. Changing only at quarter-marks is not feasible because "must react now" situations often come up, but being strategic about when the switches occur will help your efficiency and allow you to provide clear instruction to your team.

- **Last-hour:** A final check to see where production will end up, make final moves, and prepare for the hand-off to the next shift.

- **Handoff:** The time to pass the operation off to the next shift and communicate how the shift went to your manager and anyone else who is affected by your department.

Checking production is where a familiar understanding of rates comes into play. Seeing what's been done is useless without knowing whether you are on the right track to accomplish the day's goals. Rates are a good way to judge this, but you should calculate remaining work at each of the breaks throughout the shift and confirm that current staffing will work.

A good technique to track production is to keep a whiteboard in your startup area with hour or quarter increments on it to show what you planned, what happened, and why. This might look like:

Rate: 35 PPH   **Picking Production**

Hour		Staff	Planned	Actual	Delta	Notes
7:00 AM	8:00 AM	15	525	480	-45	Long startup
8:00 AM	9:00 AM	15	525	530	5	
9:00 AM	10:00 AM	15	394	400	6	Break
10:00 AM	11:00 AM	15	525	550	25	
11:00 AM	12:00 PM	15	263	230	-33	Lunch
12:00 PM	1:00 PM	13	525	450	-75	2 associates left
1:00 PM	2:00 PM	13	525	470	-55	
2:00 PM	3:00 PM	15	394	325	-69	Break; got 2 from shipping
3:00 PM	4:00 PM	15	525	460	-65	
4:00 PM	5:00 PM	15	525	440	-85	
Total			4725	4335	-390	

This type of tool (or many format variations) is helpful in monitoring progress. You can track the same information on a spreadsheet but making it public helps communicate to your team.

During the day you will be constantly communicating with your team, delivering feedback, checking on quality, monitoring your production, and dealing with any of dozens of other issues that come up. It's important to have a rhythm and plan for the entire shift so that you don't get bogged down or sidetracked.

Actions:

- Set up a standard-work checklist for yourself. This can have daily, weekly, and monthly tasks.

- Check productivity and production at regular intervals - 1st hour, quarterly, and before End-of-Shift

- Follow up with your team on productivity and quality concerns

- Adjust labor

- Prepare your handoff

- Complete the handoff to the next shift and communicate status to your manager and affected departments

End of Shift

End-of-Shift represents another transition or "seam" in the daily operation. It's not just about ceasing operations and leaving it for the next guy - it should be a deliberate process to ensure that continuity is maintained between shifts, personnel, processes, and throughput. This means that it needs to be planned and executed well.

The first part of doing a successful End-Of-Shift handoff is knowing that it's coming. It should never be a surprise that you're going to go home and give the operation to the next guy, but a lot of supervisors seem to be surprised by the fact that the shift is going to end.

The last hour is also for handoff preparation. The handoff is the transition of the operation from one set of employees to another and it is essential to keeping the flow of the operation going. As with all seams, it must be deliberately addressed to prevent the loss of critical information, discontinuity in the operation such as reduced productivity, lost product or misplaced orders, and to build trust between the teams.

If you treat it that way and leave critical details undone, the incoming shift will experience information loss and wasted time getting ramped up in the shift. This can have trickle effects when those critical details result in a service failure later on down the line. A bad handoff can create resentment from the subsequent shifts when they fail because you didn't set them up for success.

Start taking notes for your End-of-Shift handoff somewhere around the 3rd quarter of the shift, when it becomes apparent where you're going to end up and what the business is going to look like at the end of the day. Then you can determine what work has been done and what the first priorities for the next shift will be when they come in later.

The last hour is to gauge where the shift will end up and begin the process of prioritizing and setting up for the next shift's team. Make any last-minute personnel adjustments to resolve lingering problems or push on priority goals around this time. By this point the shift is already in the books, but some responsiveness can ensure that the next shift is set up for success in the handoff.

A good handoff has the following characteristics:

- Work area is clean:

    Physically. Nobody likes having to pick up after the earlier guy or hunt for job-required items.

    Process-wise: avoid handing off the deficiencies of your planning for the next shift to fix. This kind of problem tends to snowball because the business doesn't stop to let the operation recover; the operation can see ripple effects of bad planning or poor execution for days or weeks. This can include exception-handling (like damage or rework) as well as core production process status.

    Systematically: As much problem-solving has been accomplished as possible. Don't leave mystery problems that require research or lots of time for someone else to re-discover.

- Supplies are ready for the next shift - examples include RF scanners, forklifts are on chargers, carts are put back.

- The next shift has enough WIP (work-in-process) that they can immediately get to work.

- Information is passed to your manager, the next shift supervisor, and any other departments affected about production, goals, any barriers encountered, and any problems.

I **strongly** recommend walking the floor with the previous manager during the handoff to get an actual look at what is there. This will help call to mind things that they might not have written down, other situations that came up during the shift, and provide more overall context on what you are about to take responsibility for. Likewise, you should plan to be available for the next supervisor if you overlap at all.

Last, say Thank You to your people as they leave. This is important: Your employees don't have to come in on a given day, and thanking them helps keep the job human and lets them know that you - their leadership and representative of the company - care about the fact that they were there working for you.

Actions:

- Ensure that you set up a good handoff for the next shift in terms of physical setup, workflow to start, and information exchange

- Ensure your team knows the standard window allowed for ceasing work

- Walk the floor with the next supervisor

- Thank your team as they leave

Post-Shift

Great! You're done with your shift. There a few things you should do before going home.

If you have an end-of-shift report to complete, fill in the final details from your end-of-shift walk and send it out to your manager and anyone else affected. This often includes key pieces of information:

1) Safety: were there any incidents or concerns?
2) Production: what did you get done for the day?
3) Remaining work: what didn't get done that the next guy needs to look out for when he walks in?
4) Other issues: Were there process problems? Barriers to production? Opportunities or potential issues coming up? Visitors? Team member problems? This is an opportunity to recap what happened when it is still fresh in your mind, so the management team is equipped to identify and resolve the issues.

Even if an end-of-shift report is not mandatory, it is useful for capturing what you did and where you left off for your manager and any supervisors coming in. It provides a historical snapshot of what happened. If there are later questions about what went on, then you and other employees have more detail to rely on than just memory.

This is also a good time to send any requests or issues to your boss that came up during the shift. What problems or barriers are you facing? What do you need to solve them?

Last, set up your tentative staffing plan for the next day so that you only need a few adjustments when you walk in, ready for another shift.

Your Team and Essential Tools

"A leader is someone who causes people to do that which they ought to do but would not do in the absence of the leader."
- *John T Reed*

Floor Presence

What Floor Presence Is

"Floor Presence" refers to being physically out in the warehouse work area. During the shift, a strong floor presence supplements the analytics or reports for production and lets you effectively manage your team.

While reports can tell you where you are "by the numbers," observing the floor will give immense amounts of information about the process, potential problems, and what the employees are facing. It builds relationships, credibility, and trust with the team while deterring misbehavior. If you have a big enough warehouse, it can also improve your cardiovascular fitness significantly. Walking 10 miles per shift is not uncommon!

Bring your laptop while mobile through the warehouse to allow instant access to information while maintaining the critical on-floor perspective.

While on the floor, walking around without an agenda just looking at things can be very productive. Most of the time you will have specific tasks that you are trying to accomplish, whether they be finding a specific pallet, delivering feedback to a team member, doing safety checks, or researching inventory issues. However, being on the floor for the sake of being on the floor is also valuable - it puts you in touch with the process and what's happening.

Noticing and Reacting

You will become calibrated to your environment and begin to notice all sorts of things - Why is that pallet out of place? Why is the dock so full at this point in the shift? The damage area is full; Scanners aren't working well; the aisles are clogged up in the non-conveyable side of the warehouse; Cooler 3 has water on the floor; putaway quality is poor - the pallets aren't being racked correctly; the handoff is going to be rough because of all the product still sitting in the aisles. All of these things are little insights into the variables affecting your operation and could be individual issues, or could be symptomatic of larger staffing, training, or process problems. But you simply **can't** notice those things in an office. You need to be on the floor, and on the floor a lot, to understand what's happening.

Then you can do your job and ask **"why"** those things are happening, address them, and help create a better workplace for your team.

Further, you can ensure that key processes are being followed, and give on-the-spot coaching to employees. This is very effective in a setting with any process or tool changes. You can give proper guidance on the spot, in the environment, instead of trying to address hypotheticals from an employee's recollection a day or two later.

Observations and Approachability

Floor presence will also ensure your team is staying on task and on track and doing what you need them to do. You can see what people actually do on the floor - who talks in the aisles? Who is scanning multiple items at once? Are safety practices being followed? These are all valuable insights and being present lets you follow up immediately.

Being present also allows your employees to approach you directly with issues. Some employees may not want to voice concerns in a group setting like a start-up meeting and want to come straight to you. This in turn lets you snuff problems before they even become issues. If you, the first-line supervisor are right there to take on a problem, then the employee can get on with his or her job and feels like the building leadership cares and is engaged. This is the warehouse application of "MBWA" or "Management by Walking Around" - it pays big dividends in a warehouse setting. It also builds your credibility because you're out in the middle of the action, not just sitting in an office at a desk.

Tools

Having a notebook, something to take pictures with, and some way to email is very useful. I frequently carried a laptop computer with me in one facility, and a smartphone in a different facility. They were useful for photo-capturing damaged items, equipment, inventory errors, safety issues, employee concerns, and any of the dozens of other things that pop up during a day to follow up on. The point is to have something on-hand to take notes and pictures with in the moment while you are on the floor, instead of waiting until you get to a computer and forget the issue or don't follow up on the dilemma. The downsides to carrying a laptop include having to be constantly aware of battery charge levels, because running out of battery will remove your situational awareness on your operational status, and the physical burden of carrying the computer around.

How Much Floor Time?

As a general rule, plan on spending 75% or more of your time out on the floor. Get a stand-up desk in your start-up area and a laptop. Walk around with the laptop if needed. Available, well-lit, comfortable office spaces and desks are tempting. Don't fall for it. Many supervisors become anchored to a desk and convince themselves that their job demands sitting down away from their teams. This is wrong. If you want to be effective, you need to be on the floor most of the time. Otherwise, you will miss crucial production and personnel issues that you could have (and **should** have) prevented by being present on the floor.

Get Into The Process

When I created onboarding programs for my supervisors, I scheduled time for them during the first week to introduce them to the managers and work in every major process in the building for a couple hours. The first week was just that – no meetings and no emails. They showed up, participated in startups at different departments, and then working in different processes during the day.

In addition to generating some "free" production, this had several benefits:

- This introduced the new supervisors to other supervisors and managers in the building, developing a **social support group**
- The new supervisors **learned** how the product flowed through the building, and got hands-on experience with the systems and product
- The new supervisors got **credibility** with associates for having done the work

If a process happens in your area, make a point of periodically **actually doing** the process for a couple hours, even if it's not part of your daily schedule or onboarding. Get an employee to coach or train you if needed. The important part is that you're the one actually moving the product, doing the scans, typing on the computer, or whatever.

You will gain many benefits from this.

First, you'll understand how the process works. You'll handle the systems and get experiential learning, instead of just hearing about it or observing. You'll have to make the decisions that come with accomplishing the tasks. This detail is invaluable in understanding how to fix issues, improve processes, communicate opportunities, and coach employees.

Second, you'll meet the employees, and they will notice that the new supervisor is doing the process, and they will **respect** that you have done the work, even if just for a couple hours. If you can make the rates, that's even better! It is a great way to build some credibility, especially if you're coming into a new building or a new department.

Team Management

Your Attitude and Role

As a philosophy, I recommend approaching the job with an attitude of "my job is removing barriers." The associates' work is to serve the customer directly. It follows that **your** job is serve **them** by removing the barriers preventing them from doing great work. Your manager should be supporting you in the same way.

It's also important to "assume positive intent" in your employees. That way you are aligned with them. You are both working together for a common goal. If you believe that most employees try to do a good job and be productive, then if they are not performing to the standard, there must be a barrier to performance. Barriers can be problems with the process, the tools, the team, direction, communication, or any other issues that are getting in the way of performance. Often if an employee is experiencing a problem of some sort - say, insufficient training - then you have also identified an issue that is negatively affecting the entire group. If you correct it then you will see better overall results.

Once you remove the barriers that prevent the individual from determining his own outcomes, then individual performance management enters the picture. But your first reaction to a problem shouldn't be to blame an employee for poor performance. First, look at what might be inhibiting the performance. Fix those issues, and then look to the individual.

Motivating

Whole other books are written on motivating teams, and it is an important part of the warehouse supervisor's job. Part of setting the standard for your employees includes having the proper mindset to accomplish the day's goals and motivating the team. While you don't have to be artificially happy, you should be able to put a positive feeling on the day and the work. Remind the team about the customer to keep them focused on the importance of the day-to-day tasks.

Different individuals require different approaches for motivation, but nobody appreciates being lied to, misdirected, unappreciated, or uninformed. People like knowing what they do matters, that they are helping someone, and that they are doing a good job, or at least improving. If you let your team know what is going on to the best of your ability, and put context around what is happening, then although they may not like what's happening you will still have their trust.

I had a critical insight when I realized that many hourly employees approach their jobs like a craft. They respect people who understand what "actually" goes on. Pickers, for instance, will have intimate knowledge of the facility and systems that affect their process. If you pay them the compliment of respecting their work and understanding the minutiae of what they do, they will be motivated to do it well, and bring up any problems or issues.

Good ways to start motivating include regular interaction with people, knowing their names, and paying attention to the issues they face. I also try to keep them informed about **why** what they're doing matters, and the impacts they have on the business. Recognition for even "small" things well-done is also an important part of the motivational arsenal. If the only time someone sees you is when you hand out write-ups, then you're missing out on opportunities to build rapport and trust.

Finally, a consistent positive attitude, a sense of mission, and a willingness to engage on issues will keep your team engaged. I made a point of consciously flipping on my personal "motivational" switch when I got out of my car and headed in the warehouse, no matter what my personal attitude was at that moment. I used to walk around telling team members that "Your customers love you!" to remind them that they directly engaged with the customer and weren't just "moving another box." A negative or defeatist attitude translates directly to poor motivation for your team.

Communicating the "Why"s of the Business

Policy: Policy-making is opaque to employees, often communicated at the last minute, and the intent may not be clear. If it looks like employees are getting screwed, they will quickly pick up on it. You need to understand where the policy is coming from and be able to explain why the policy exists. If you're not getting that information, then you have a great opportunity to give some upward feedback to your boss - "I need some help developing the message to the team about this change..." or "I don't have the information I need to communicate this effectively."

Business decisions: Decisions about how the business is run and the external environment are not often well communicated to the employees. You can keep them engaged by relaying and translating information about the competitive environment, the company's position, recent market news, or internal initiatives. **Do** let them know what's going on; don't speculate, and **don't promise anything that you are not personally committed to delivering**. I can't stress this enough: If you do not personally and perfectly understand everything that is going on **and** control it enough to be able to deliver on what you say will happen, don't promise it. You will be made a liar as soon as the company institutes a new policy or sets a new operational schedule or whatever.

General Information: If you know why a process is designed a certain way because you emailed the team responsible for the process, you can talk to your employees about it. If you find out trivia about the business or background information on OSHA requirements that affect their jobs, then talk to your employees about it. If you keep information flowing to them, they will be more informed and understand that you are working to keep them abreast of the latest news affecting their jobs. It's more humanizing than solely emphasizing production every day.

Treat Your Team Like People

This sounds obvious – your team is made up of real people. However, it's easy to forget and to instead see them as somewhat autonomous machines that do things when you tell them to. The fact that your people have desires, needs, strengths, weaknesses, and outside lives should never be far from your mind. You demonstrate this by listening, understanding, respecting, and advocating for your team, even though as the supervisor you represent the business and must maintain some professional and authority distance.

Advocating for the Team

You have a seat at the management table and should advocate for your team. Although you are a manager and have a primary responsibility to the business, the employees are part of that business. Raising legitimate employee-raised issues for resolution will win you great credibility both with your employees and the rest of the management group.

Follow-Up

One of the most difficult parts of team leadership is following up on commitments or requests. If you commit to someone that you will do something, remember to do it - and then let the employee know what you did. This is difficult because you will be bombarded on any given day with a dozen requests for help, or to look at something, or complaints - and it's your responsibility to follow up on all of it! Taking notes and then letting the employee what you did (or didn't) do on the issue lets them know that you listened and did what you could to address the issue. Even if the answer is not what the employee wanted, the follow-up will be appreciated.

There are other types of follow-up. If you notice something that is not up to standard, you owe it to your team to give them specific, actionable feedback. If you let unsatisfactory performance continue, that is your fault. The employee may not be performing, but you're not correcting the situation, and trying to hold them responsible way after the fact – like at a review period months after you noticed the problem – is irresponsible. If you have an issue with something, bring it up in a professional manner as soon as you can identify the problem so that you can understand it and offer guidance to address it. More of this will be discussed in the coaching sections below.

This is reflected in the trust that your employees have in you and the credibility that you have. It contributes to the perception of management's competence and connection with the employees, and you are that link.

Understanding Performance Standards

Most distribution organizations have performance standards. Those standards are commonly set in rates of things-per-hour and are used as proxies for cost. They form the basis of production planning and eventually to the overall organization budget. They are very important to whether the building "makes money." Part of your responsibilities will be to manage the performance of the employees that are not performing to the standard.

You should understand where those numbers come from, and how they are adjusted. Some are from a percentile performance standard of the employees. Others are educated guesses about historical output. Regardless, when you are performance managing someone, you should have an idea why the rate is the rate.

In some cases, you may be in an organization that doesn't have a uniform enough process to have performance standards, or the tools for measuring don't exist. In those cases, you may have to build tools or yardsticks to gauge what productivity looks like. The important thing is having a consistent standard to refer to. Doing performance management for someone without standards to operate from is very difficult. Even though that person may be deliberately the slowest person on the team, performance management will be very difficult unless you are aware of both the performance and the standards.

Setting Performance Standards

If the standards are not common knowledge or provided in a company document, then you need to ensure that everyone is aware of the standards. Communication during start-up meetings is important and posting them in a public place such as start-up area or break room will ensure that they are public knowledge. This will prevent any team members from claiming ignorance of the performance measures. Posting periodic lists of performance by individual is also a technique for keeping employees appraised of their performance. This can create a competitive atmosphere as some will strive to be the best. Others will not care if they are making the minimum rate. The employees at the bottom will have constant access to a performance ranking and if you make it a documented practice to post performance numbers, they will never be caught off guard.

Performance standards are often built from aggregate employee performance over time and scaled to be achievable. For example, some models take individual average performance over a series of weeks, scale the performance distribution to a normal distribution, and set a performance goal at some percentile of performance. If you don't know how your organization's performance standards were developed, go ask someone. You need to understand where the numbers come from, and be able to explain them to your team, because they need to know that the standards are both necessary for the business, and that they are achievable.

Quality standards are more difficult to quantify, but there are a few ways to think about them. The first is also in terms of rates: An employee can have a certain rate of errors before getting coached. The second is in terms of absolute errors, where certain types of errors receive coaching. Quality errors take more effort to identify and research but are often the errors that are really holding your shift back and causing your customers the most pain.

Communicate the Standards

Once you have standards for performance, ensure that those standards are publicly known. Talking about the standards at startup meetings and posting expectations and performance are good ways of ensuring that your employees know the expectation and how they are performing.

You gain nothing from hiding information on the standards from the team, and they won't feel unfairly treated when you follow up with them on their performance.

Coaching to Performance Standards

Coaching to performance is straightforward. If you have a set of expectations for a given process, and some consistent underperformance by an employee, you should coach them on their performance. This should be a regular review - weekly works well - and depending on your facility you may want to actually explain how the evaluation system works to your employees so they know what to expect.

The rates or actual performance outputs are commonly accessible through the various computer systems and reports that the company has. Daily throughput and shift length per individual are enough to measure performance over time.

There is some ambiguity about what "consistent" underperformance means. The period of time in the process should be long enough to give the employee an opportunity to hit average rates. If the employee was put into a particularly difficult process for a day and doesn't hit the rate, that is a different coaching situation than if the employee was rotated through jobs for a week and did not hit the rate. You can expect to hear many reasons why the employee did not make the performance goal, so it is important that the sample of performance be large enough that it is representative of the employee's whole work.

A good remedy for performance problems is to observe (or have a trainer observe) the employee in process. This can yield insights about the employee's pace/sense of urgency, ergonomics, setup and preparation, familiarity with the process, or other techniques which can be used to coach the employee to a productive pace. If the employee demonstrates that he can meet the expectation under observation, then he is well positioned to meet the standard in general. As always, documenting the trainings is useful if the performance issues continue.

Coaching to Quality Standards

Managing quality standards or performance in accuracy is different than performance. More research is required to figure out what caused the quality problem. Some issues are purely behavioral, as when the employee doesn't follow a documented process with all available tools, resulting in quality errors. It becomes more complicated when the issue is that the tools or methods weren't available to the employee, and the employee had to improvise to accomplish the task. In that case, assuming positive intent is a good approach and coaching the employee to ask for help is a good solution.

To proactively manage concerns, you should have a good idea of what happens in your process and what is required for it to work properly. For example, if your employees are using RF guns, do all locations have scannable barcodes or are they typing the codes for missing labels? It is hard to correct an employee for quality if the setting is forcing him to not follow a process that is designed to minimize mistakes.

If all tools are available and the employee is still not following the process, resulting in quality errors, then corrective action should follow.

Exemptions

You will need to advocate for your employees as often as performance manage them. Strict rates and numbers built from averages do not factor in special assignments or uniquely difficult circumstances that employees may face. When one of those becomes apparent, you can and should argue for exemptions from the regular performance standard, but only with solid evidence of why the exemption is deserved - solid enough that you could make the case in front of all of your hourly employees. Otherwise you will be effectively treating employees differently, which is favoritism and which will degrade the team's trust in you.

Number-One Cause Of Accuracy and Quality Errors

Violating "one-piece-flow" – also known as "batching" or "Machine-gunning" a process – is the number one cause of errors. Most processes are designed to be done one-piece-of-work-at-a-time. If the employee starts "batching" work, then he will have errors. This can apply in scanning ahead on items, doing putaway on multiple items at once, trying to pick 20 items by scanning one label and typing in the quantity, or scanning items ahead of physically receiving them. It's much harder to have errors when completing one piece of work at a time, but it feels slower to the employee, resulting in temptation to do multiple items at once.

Combating batching is a behavioral effort. You have to convince your employees through messaging as well as research and follow-up on violations. If your process systems are built to support it, they can also help identify and ensure that employees are following one-piece-flow by requiring multiple individual system steps, but if they are not configured that way then you will have to do it yourself.

In your computer systems, this can be identified by looking at time-stamps for each of the transactions in the process filtered by user. Timestamps that are very close together may very well indicate violations of one-piece flow. Extraordinarily high productivity and high error rates will also give you some initial places to look for one-piece-flow violations.

A useful tool in quality, as with productivity, is posting accuracy and quality rates if you have access to that information. This will again inspire some competition and will keep everybody apprised of their performance well in advance of any coaching or corrective conversations that you need to have.

How to Have A Coaching Conversation

Having coaching conversations about productivity or quality is often stressful for supervisors, and a lot of people avoid them. But remember: You're providing feedback to help the employee succeed. You're seeking to identify problems, and then help solve those problems. Nobody likes to hear that they're not doing well, but often employees want to succeed, and appreciate feedback or a constructive partnering approach on how to do better. If they don't, then you're doing your job to the business by coaching and progressing them. And delaying delivering these messages does not make the problems go away; it makes them worse, later.

Identify the goal of the conversation
You will have a goal or end to the conversation that you want to achieve. Try to articulate it before actually having the

conversation, so you know where you want to end up without getting distracted or off topic.

Research ahead of time
Have adequate detail and facts to understand the situational context before having the conversation. That can mean research on system records for attendance or performance, or other details that might bear on the situation. There is a big difference between going into a conversation knowing some details about what happened and having to discover them on the spot as the employee - whose job is affected by getting write-ups - points out things that you should have noticed or asked about before the conversation. Specific examples are essential here; numbers help, and so do specific observations.

Conduct the Seek-to-Understand Conversation
A "Seek-to-Understand" conversation is just that: You want to confirm what happened and understand why. This should be the first step in any corrective or coaching conversation. Many times performance issues, given a little more context, reveal important insights about the process. Sometimes the current research indicates actual individual behavioral issues that need correcting, but you want to be sure. *"Bob, it looks from this system record that you had 28 minutes between scans. What was going on?"* is much more effective than *"Bob, you were slow last week, so you're getting a productivity write-up."* The former approach will identify the issue and build trust that you're on their side; the latter will build an adversarial environment.

Identify barriers, commit to follow-up
As part of the conversation you will often discover that there were circumstances affecting the work performance. These may or not be pertinent to the coaching, but you should understand why the issues exist and how they affect your team.

"Bob, I understand that you were waiting for a new cart to be built for putaway, like the trainer told you to. To clarify, the process is that if there's not a cart at your divert, then you should check the next nearest divert for work instead of waiting. Can you do that in the future? Great. And I'll follow up with the trainer on the right way to do it, and we'll announce it at startup."

If you learn of something you can affect, take notes and commit to following up - then do it.

Set expectations
If the barriers are employee-controlled (e.g. the employee isn't doing what he's supposed to), then you can set expectations for dealing with those in the future. Language might include "So from now on, I expect that you [do whatever]" or "The standard is X, and you need to meet that or let me know what's going on as it's happening so I can help."

Get acknowledgment
An important part of the conversation is verifying that the employee understands what is going on. Getting acknowledgment and capturing it indicates that you weren't talking into a vacuum. And if you were, that's worth documenting too. "Does that make sense? Is it realistic? Will you do that?" are good questions to prompt responses.

Wrap it up
Don't linger too long. Do the conversation, be receptive to concerns, and get the employee back into process instead of dwelling on it.

Document: Send a record of the conversation to HR or however your company tracks feedback and correctives.

An example summary might read:
"I had a conversation with Joe at 3PM on July 19th to follow up about his quality. We talked at the lead's desk, and I pointed out that his accuracy rates over the last three weeks were all below expectation. I reviewed each week's accuracy report with him and some specific error examples where he had consistently mislabeled the product. Joe said that he had trouble distinguishing the Size A products from the Size B products. I let him know that those products were most of our business, and that he would need to become more familiar with the product to get his accuracy up to the standard. I also noted that his scan record indicated that he was processing multiple labels at once, which could lead to errors. Joe said he understood and wouldn't do that any more. I offered to get Training to review labeling and product types with him. Joe accepted the feedback and training offer and thanked me for the help. I committed to having the retraining scheduled for completion by next Tuesday."

How to Document the Conversation

A few quick actions will ensure that you are prepared and conclude the issue:

- Have notes ahead of time on the key points you need to address. These can include performance numbers or specific behavioral examples.

- Ensure you hit the key points of the notes

- Recap points and form of conversation in email to HR or on the appropriate forms.

Good Warehousing Practices

What Good Warehousing Is

Each operation has its own standard set of "good warehousing practices." There are some universal items to check for on your team to ensure that you are running a quality operation in a good working environment.

General Practices to check and audit include:

Scan as you go: Always scan what you move. If your team is not scanning at the proper points in their regular operations, you will see quality and accuracy problems. Look into records of employees with quality or accuracy issues. If there aren't scannable locations where you're moving product, notify your manager or whoever configures your warehouse to set some up.

One Piece Flow: Do one piece of work at a time. If your team is batching actions when they're not supposed to be, you will see quality problems. How do you identify this? Pull up activity records or reports from your WMS by user and compare the timestamps to what you should be seeing if they were following the process. Audits of employees with quality or accuracy problems will probably yield actionable discoveries.

Audit The Process: Check your process outputs for quality and accuracy. Log the errors you find for record-keeping and follow-up.

Verify Product and Labels: Read the label; read the product; escalate discrepancies. This can be difficult for an employee to do, but it's a habit that you can help build. Keep in mind that your employees are probably spending 10 or 12 hours per day moving product. After a while, picking hundreds of cases of a product means that they will tend to make assumptions to speed the process up. This might not even be conscious; their brains might simply not notice detail differences among all the similarities between product (for instance, picking similar sizes of softlines, different package counts or datelots of similar product, etc). However, as with completing correct flow processes, this is extremely important, and quality errors should lead you to point out and coach these errors.

Label control: Labels store information. Missing labels are lost information. Duplicate labels lead to mistakes that cannot be caught by the system. If you see labels on the floor, your team is probably not controlling their information well, and it is likely that you will see accuracy problems caused by double-tagging or lack of tags. This is a difficult error to identify until the problem has occurred, because an active tag allows product to be processed through the system, albeit to incorrect places.

Housekeeping: Clean as you go. As with other safety-related issues, this is extremely important but often neglected in the heat of a production environment. Warehouses tend to accumulate debris due to the mass amounts of material movement, packaging and securement fragmentation, damage, heavy machinery, and hard-to-reach areas. Cleaning takes time, but if your team is not doing it, then start communicating the importance. Setting expectations for housekeeping and establishing regular cleaning routines are the first step. Coaching and incentives may be required to get your employees to buy in, and your leadership team should also be aligned on this. The outcome will be a floor that looks neat and organized, prevents equipment damage, prevents slip/trip/fall hazards conditions, improved product accountability, and is a place that people are comfortable working in.

Human Resources and Administration

Human Resources is an interesting function in any building and can be either a tremendous asset or impediment to what you're trying to do.

What you're trying to do at a fundamental level is remove barriers to a high-performing operation. To do this you need to make sure your team can perform. As part of that, you need to make sure the right people are in place (or at least that the wrong people aren't in place) and that they have the right incentives to perform.

Administration

There is not really a good place to put this topic, but it does deserve some ink since it will consume a significant part of your time and attention. Supervisors are often required to complete administrative tasks related to their teams. This often includes managing Personal Time Off (PTO) requests, scheduling overtime, approving vacation, reviewing timecards and clock punches, reviewing and submitting lists of employees who meet this or that criteria, helping address pay issues, administering leaves of absence, reviewing system access, setting system permissions, creating performance plans, administering documented coachings and corrective progressions, terminating employees, training employees, and on and on. All of this comes with 'paperwork' and time and attention.

This is all important to ensuring that your employees are treated well and fairly, that they're paid for the work they do, and that the business has good processes in place. My recommendation is to schedule consistent time in your day to address the repetitive administrative tasks, set 'office hours' for Associates to see you during the shift with exceptions, and to communicate proactively. If you don't maintain good control of the administration of your team members' issues, you'll fail them and your company.

HR is a Tool

The first thing to realize about HR is that it is a tool for the company to use. It should not, ideally, support either management or employees over the other; its job is protecting the company and promoting the company's interests.

Given that, you can expect HR to play by a very defined playbook. Policy and procedure, fairness and equity, and a risk management mindset will dominate the department.

As a supervisor, you have two options: You can ignore HR o0r be befuddled and stymied by it or understand the rulebook and learn to work in the system. This means understanding the policies and regulatory environment that you and your company operate in.

How to Use HR Teams

Some actions you must learn to take include:

- Documenting conversations, occurrences, and coachings

It's easy to document, but it's much easier to not-document. However, not documenting is a form of what Ben Horowitz calls "Management Debt"; it may be easier and save time now, but it will accrue "interest" when you are forced to re-do the work later, or put up with sub-standard performance from someone whom you should have performance-managed earlier.

- Asking questions and making allies

Partner with your HR staff early on all issues affecting people. Ask their opinions on impacts regarding operational issues in dealing with people. This doesn't mean you have to do what they say, but they will feel integrated into your decision process and you can influence them on key issues early. This becomes helpful in dealing with problem employees and ensuring you are following policy early as issues develop instead of trying to catch up after the problem is apparent, like when they're suing you.

- Informing early about concerns

As mentioned, get HR involved early in potential problems with people as you identify them. Once you have identified the issue, email or face-to-face chats about the concern and what options are available will again set you up for minimal wasted effort and less time dealing with the problem effectively.

- Forming your own staffing strategy

As you assess your team for strong and weak performers you will build an idea of what changes you want to make to the team. Having that vision in mind and then going to HR with some clearly identified goals for development or team-improvement will get you all on the same page. Often HR will have ideas on how to progress that strategy which you can use to build the team instead of letting the current situation continue.

Poor HR Support Infrastructure

When I started, I considered HR to be a department that, now and again, would tell me that I couldn't do something or remind me to get some training. However, after working with a few good HR managers and teams, I realized that they can be tremendous assets in developing systems and processes to manage performance and culture.

But sometimes you will have an HR department that is not helpful - an HR team may not have any insights on team management or how to resolve problems, or they get so stuck on process that there is no way to make progress with the team or site. Common symptoms of this would be if HR requires excessive documentation and cannot present options or a roadmap of how to achieve goals in performance management or culture, or if other barriers seem excessively burdensome to deal with. This may be due to company requirements, but the local team should know how to navigate those effectively.

An effective way of coping with this situation is to let your supervisor or manager know what you want to do - being proactive with your communication will go a long way - and then proceeding to follow the correct steps yourself and override HR. In that case, you have a higher obligation to your team and to the business than to following the whims of someone who may not be an expert in either his own area of responsibility or yours.

Being stymied by an incompetent HR department is not an adequate reason to be held back.

If your management won't facilitate getting things done, then either accept the situation, or quit and get a job where someone will support the operation.

Pitfalls

Common pitfalls from a Supervisor point of view include not partnering with HR early and often on issues that come up, not documenting, and not following up on employee concerns. If an employee raises a concern that's not purely process-related, it does not hurt to inform HR about the conversation. Any time a fairness, compensation, time, or other issue comes up, HR should probably know, if only to help keep a good feeling of the pulse in the building.

Further, in intelligence, there is something called "mosaic theory." This is the idea that a single bit of information may be useless by itself but combined with other information can paint a very comprehensive picture of what is happening. HR is often in a position to collect bits of information from throughout the building, across all departments, at all levels. This lets the HR folks understand wide trends about what is happening and help address big issues before they become bigger issues. This is another good reason to let HR know what is happening, even if it might seem minor.

A proactive approach with HR and keeping them informed about what goals you are working for will keep you aligned and on track with achieving those goals.

Actions:

- **Document:** Carry around a notebook during the day. Keep notes on all coaching conversations with employees. Email HR a summary of those conversations toward the end of the day. This ensures that dated records of coachings - even if not used for corrective purposes - are on file for any future reference.

- **Engage**: Regularly talk with your HR folks about your team and where you see it going. Let them know of incidents or conversations that occurred that might be "of interest."

Managing For Yourself

Now you've gotten the hang of managing your shift, your associates, and working with the rest of the building. What's left?

Being a supervisor lays great groundwork for your future. It's important to put full effort into taking everything out of your current role that you can, because it will be your reference to how to manage people, processes, systems, and equipment. It will give you perspective on the every-day challenges that the teams face as they "make it happen."

But you also may not want to be a supervisor forever. If that's the case, there are a few things you should be doing to prepare yourself for next steps. They include self-initiated education, development, and upward management.

Education: Read about all aspects of your job; be voracious. Moving materials is a huge industry and challenge, especially as delivery times get shorter and the data driving the business gets more granular and accurately employed. Operations Management and Warehousing has practitioners that devote significant parts of their careers to things like engineering (from capacity management down to detailed pieces of knowledge like how to construct strong pallets), material-handling systems, automation, industrial psychology, HR information systems, general management, operations research, analytics, sales and solutions, and so on. Learning about these things will make you more effective and employable in other capacities.

Development: Set one-on-one meetings with your supervisor, maybe once every week or every other week. Send an agenda to your supervisor a day ahead of the meeting, and discuss your shift's performance in metrics, achievements, opportunities, and projects. Ask for feedback, and then follow up on that feedback. This will indicate your willingness to learn and provide regular updates to your supervisor on accomplishments and challenges. It gives you a venue for discussing opportunities to build your career. Ultimately, this builds rapport with your supervisor, and you can set similar introductory meetings with other management in the company to learn about different parts of the business and build your personal brand.

Upward Management: Your boss is a person too, with her own responsibilities. She is responsible for another set of metrics, your performance, keeping her boss informed, managing resources and hiring, and strategic projects. You can help her do her job by pushing information, seeking counsel, and being proactive in operating. Surfacing problems early, taking action and informing, and giving her the tools she needs to manage effectively are a way to manage upward to ensure a smooth relationship. Don't be afraid to initiate communication with emails, meetings, or through other venues to push communication upward. Nobody likes to be surprised, and even though you may feel that "it's not important," it's probably worth pushing the information or asking questions.

Conclusion

Warehousing is conceptually very simple - after all, you're just moving boxes, right? - but doing it well requires organization, discipline, and juggling multiple operational priorities with effective personal relationships. You are running a business within a business. Personal growth opportunities come from attaining high levels of basic proficiency at the topics in this book, and then looking deeper into your processes to understand what's going on at multiple levels of causation and incentives.

All that gets you onto the floor, with your team, ready to look at what you have to do, how you have to do it, and gives some approaches to doing it well. I hope that reading this handbook got you oriented in the correct direction and looking at the right things to succeed as a supervisor. You can have a tremendous impact on your team and your building. Good luck!

Resources

This handbook drew not only on personal experiences and observations but also on lessons learned from some other operations literature. Most of the references I found useful are focused specifically on warehousing, Lean process methodology, and people management. The most useful works are below.

High Output Management: By Andy Grove, the former Intel CEO. This is a collection of general management practices including general operations understanding, people management, and talent management. This should be mandatory reading for managers as it covers many best practices of general people management, like how to coach people and get the best performance you can from them. I buy copies of this one for my operations managers. It's that good.

2-Second Lean: By Paul Akers. This is a useful primer for incremental Lean improvements without being as dense as The Toyota Way. The main insight I took from this is that small, incremental improvements are available in many settings, and that driving the culture with a team takes visible and concrete steps.

The Goal: This "business classic" by Eli Goldratt talks through identifying and understanding bottlenecks in production, or "constraints," and is presented in novel format. It is useful for framing how to identify process issues related to constraints and pull-production systems, and what to do about some of them.

Learning to See: Value Stream Mapping to Add Value and Eliminate Muda: By Mike Rother and John Shook. Process Improvement book on how to value-stream map and identify waste in processes. This is very easy to read, has illustrations, and is a good general reference for helping to understand what is actually happening in your facility.

The Toyota Way: 14 Management Principles from the World's Greatest Manufacturer: By Jeffrey Liker. This is the work on understanding the building-blocks of the Lean Production System and how they might apply in your organization and facility. I recommend it to inform your view of what's really value-added in your processes, and where there may be barriers to and waste in your team's work affecting both quality and productivity.

Warehouse Supervisor's Standard Manual: Put out by the Prentice Hall Bureau of Business Practice. This is a collection of tools for supervisors, published in 1983, with an emphasis on the human-relations aspect of management. It has a variety of approaches and anecdotes for preparing supervisors to deal with the day-to-day issues that employees raise, from perception management, to staffing, to overtime management and some productivity management tools. It's out of print and hard to find. This was the only other book I found specifically on this topic.

Warehouse Management: A Complete Guide to Improving Efficiency and Minimizing Costs in a Modern Warehouse: By Gwynne Richards. A high-level, comprehensive resource on warehousing practices and tools for the distribution/warehousing professional. It covers warehouse configuration, inventory management, equipment selection, environmental considerations, employee management, and cost reduction and productivity measurement and actions. Very thorough, very in-depth, and very long.

World Class Warehousing and Material Handling: By Ed Frazelle. This is an "encyclopedia" of warehousing and process design. It covers order profiling, warehouse design consideration, and multiple techniques for warehouse processes from receiving through shipping. It is a must-read for distribution professionals.

About the Author

Paul Lukehart grew up in Bakersfield, California and attended West Point and Harvard Business School. He has worked in warehousing distribution roles from supervisor through director. His industry experience includes in-house distribution for retail and e-commerce businesses and third-party logistics in produce, appliances, apparel/footwear, and reverse logistics. He has operated and managed distribution center multiple start-ups. As of this writing, Paul resides in Indiana and welcomes ideas, suggestions, or feedback for this guide at p.lukehart@gmail.com.

Made in the USA
Columbia, SC
21 August 2023

21940729R00064